More praise for *Adrift*

"There have been many tales of survival, but *Adrift* is twenty thousand leagues over the rest. . . . For aficionados of sailing literature, Callahan's story is to William F. Buckley's *Atlantic High* as the Great Chicago Fire is to cuddling up in front of a cozy hearth. . . . Callahan is, besides being an adept sailor, a fine writer, who can find universals in his situation where others might be paralyzed with fear."

—*Kirkus Reviews*

"Callahan's vivid depiction and candid thoughts make this book utterly captivating—a real page-turner."

—*Booklist*

"This is real human drama that delves deeply into a man's survival instincts. It should be read by anyone venturing offshore in a small boat."

—*Library Journal*

STEVEN CALLAHAN

ILLUSTRATIONS BY THE AUTHOR

Ballantine Books • New York

ADRIFT

SEVENTY-SIX DAYS LOST AT SEA

Copyright © 1986 by Steven Callahan

All rights reserved under International and Pan-American Copyright Conventions. Published in the United States by Ballantine Books, a division of Random House, Inc., New York, and simultaneously in Canada by Random House of Canada Limited, Toronto.

http://www.randomhouse.com

Library of Congress Catalog Card Number: 96-96655

ISBN: 0-345-41015-7

First published by Houghton Mifflin Company. Reprinted by permission of Houghton Mifflin Company.

Manufactured in the United States of America

First Ballantine Books Mass Market Edition: May 1987
First Ballantine Books Trade Edition: August 1996

10 9 8 7 6 5

This book is dedicated to people everywhere
who know, have known, or will know
suffering, desperation,
or loneliness.

CONTENTS

ᏍᏍᎷᎩ ACKNOWLEDGMENTS

A huge number of people played a role in the creation of this book, directly and indirectly. First, there are those who introduced me to sailing and taught me the skills that enabled me to survive my experience: I am especially grateful to my parents and to the people of the Boy Scouts organization, particularly Arthur Adams. My ex-wife, Frisha Hugessen, was very supportive and tolerant of my projects, including the building of *Napoleon Solo,* while Chris Latchem helped me to achieve my goals and to develop techniques for confronting practical problems.

I am grateful to Dougal Robertson for his excellent survival manual, *Sea Survival,* which unfortunately is out of print. The Robertsons, the Baileys, and other voyagers who went before me kept me company through their books and provided not only essential practical advice but also the inspiration to pull through.

I might not ever have made it ashore had it not been for my timely meeting with the Paquet brothers and Paulinus Williams. They and the other people of Marie Galante were very kind and helpful during the final stage of my voyage and my subsequent recovery.

Kathy Massimini gave me an unbelievable amount of moral support and editorial advice throughout the writing of this book. Every author probably relies on someone like Kathy to pull him through the hard times and keep him on track, but I can't believe there are that many people out there with as much faith, tolerance, and insight.

Harry Foster, my editor at Houghton Mifflin, put a great deal of faith in me and guided me with a firm hand and patient ear.

I would also like to acknowledge all the people who aided in SAR operations and who kept circulating information and messages about me and *Solo* even after official channels were closed. In addition they gave my family a great deal of moral support. Among the many I would like to thank are the amateur and CB radio network, William Wanklyn, Francis Carter, *Sail* magazine's staff, Hood Sailmakers, Oscar Fabian Gonzales, the Steggalls, Beth Pollock, Hayden Brown, *Cruising World*'s staff, the late Phil Weld, Mathias Achoun, his friend Freddie, and Maurice Briand. There are many others. I must also thank my family for their efforts in trying to locate me and keeping faith.

Finally, I would like to express my gratitude to the sea. It has taught me quite a lot in life. Although the sea was my greatest enemy, it was also my greatest ally. I know intellectually that the sea is indifferent, but her richness allowed me to survive. In giving up her dorados, she was giving up her own children, so to speak, in order that I might live.

I truly hope that the remainder of my life will prove worthy of all the sacrifices made on my behalf.

PREFACE

This story is a true one. It is now three years after the event. Some aspects of the voyage were more important and produced stronger images at the time than they do now. For instance, weather is one of the most potent forces encountered by mariners, as it is for others who work directly with the environment—farmers, divers, mountain climbers. On land we hardly notice a low-pressure system that scatters rain and blows thirty-five miles an hour. It's simple for us to don a raincoat and hop from our house to our car to our office building. Offshore, the effects of weather are greatly amplified. Winds of thirty-five knots in the Atlantic can cause dangerous waves: in shoal waters and in areas of strong currents, I've seen twenty-five-foot breakers rear up. Even for relatively large vessels, such as trawlers, such conditions can be perilous. Encountering a rogue wave during such times almost guarantees disaster. Even slight increases in the weather are immediately noticed: your vessel heels over, the apparent temperature drops, your coffee leaps out of its cup. Calming trends are just as apparent: the sails flop, the rig slams around, the apparent temperature rockets from 50° to 90°. The smaller the vessel, the more sensitive it is to such shifts. Unfortunately I cannot now remember all of the nuances in the weather when I was aboard my raft. The same is true of some other details of the voyage. I often have vivid memories—say, of the way the ocean felt one day—but I don't always know which day that was. The events related here have been reconstructed from the very detailed logs that I kept. Still, these do not always record routine circumstances in detail. I have tried to capture the overall feeling or essence of each event, but I am sure that the descriptions are often inadequate to convey a real sense of what was happening.

My notations in the text that concern the SAR (search and rescue) operations of my family and the Coast Guard come from several sources. Most of the references have been crosschecked with the Coast Guard's SAR log and official letters, or my family's SAR log. A few references are from family sources only, though they usually have been verified by third parties.

Some things have become clearer as time goes on, and my perspective on the events of three years ago has evolved since returning to shore life. Yet in writing this book, I wanted to relate my experience not as I see it now but as I felt about it then. At the time, events seemed to progress in a cohesive way. As I prepared the outline for my book, I divided notations from my log into two categories: events and ideas. Under events I wrote down the details of the ships I saw, the fish I caught, the sharks I encountered, and so forth. Under ideas I wrote what I felt and thought about these events. From this I organized chapters that corresponded to the different stages of the voyage I perceived at the time. Of course, I can never be completely sure that all my conclusions are exactly what I felt then rather than new insights.

One thing I have had to come to terms with is that my experience can never be accurately portrayed. The truth of my story is like one of Plato's forms, the perfect model after which the imperfect representation in reality is fashioned. After my return, many people wrote about my story. Some tied Christian dogma to it, others romantic adventure, others Hollywood hype. This was fine by me. Even my own rendition is but an imperfect representation of what I experienced.

In many ways that is a good thing. If I could convey the true horror I felt at the time, no one would want to read this story. I have not said on every line that I was in pain and felt desperate. In telling my story, I discuss things rationally and even make jokes. I talk about myself as if my body and my emotions were separate from my rational self, but of course they could not be entirely, and no part of myself was ever free from the pain and desperation. Then, too, if I were to insist constantly on the awfulness of the situation, it would make for boring reading. The experience was too bad to be boring at the time; but readers should keep in mind that much of the survival experience is repetitive and horrible at the same time that it has its lighter, reflective, and instructive moments.

One of the most frequent questions that I'm asked is, "Do you still sail after all that?" My reply is simply, "What else would I do?" After a decade of doing nothing but messing around in boats, I cannot imagine suddenly launching a career as an astrophysicist or a Bowery bum. The sea is my work place, my playground, and my home. It has offered me a pathway to more disciplines than I can ever master. Oceanography, aerodynamics, astronomy, and common-sense problem solving are essential parts of sailing; hydrodynamics, physics, engineering, and intuitive extrapolation are essential to boat design; craftsmanship, metallurgy, forestry, and plastics technology are ingredients of boatbuilding. I am a jack-of-all-trades who has a passion for exploration. Where else can I find a place where knowing very little about a lot of things is so useful? Where else can I find such a great frontier within such easy reach?

INTRODUCTION

It is always difficult to decide where a story begins and where it ends. However, some experiences—a romantic evening, a weekend retreat, or a voyage—have fairly distinct dividing lines. They are what I call "whole experiences." To a large degree, the first twenty-nine years of my life represent one whole experience that rests outside the scope of this book. But within those years are the seeds of this story. People often ask me how I got myself into such a fix in the first place. How did I know what to do? Was the boat I lost new or had it been tried before? Why was I sailing offshore in such a small boat? The answers to these questions *are* an integral part of the story, its foundation. The foundation was laid in 1964, when, at age twelve, I began sailing.

I fell in love with sailing instantly. I can think of a million reasons why it appealed to me so strongly—the immediate relationship with the environment, the simplified lifestyle devoid of "modern inconveniences" (as naval architect Dick Newick puts it), the sheer beauty of it—but all of the reasons can be summed up succinctly: everything about it felt right.

Before I ever began to sail, I thought that if I had lived in the 1700s I would probably have become a mountain man, or some such thing. Then I became enthralled with the history of the sailing ship, of square-riggers battling their way around Cape Horn. I yearned for the romanticism and adventure of ages past. Shortly after I began sailing, I read a book called *Tinkerbelle*, by Robert Manry. In June 1965 Manry had sailed his 13.5-foot boat across the Atlantic in seventy-eight days, a record at the time. Something about the simplicity of Manry's boat, and his accomplishment of so much with so little, struck a chord in my heart. He showed me that a life of adventure was still possible in the latter part of the twentieth century.

From that time on I dreamed of crossing the Atlantic in a small boat. As years went by I learned the skills necessary to accomplish this goal. I read books about all of the great voyages: the raft crossings of the Pacific by Heyerdahl and Willis, and the circumnavigations of Slocum, the Hiscocks, and Guzzwell. Before I was out of high school, I had helped to build a forty-footer; by 1974 I had begun a boatbuilding career and was living aboard; by 1977 I was designing boats and venturing offshore as far as Bermuda; by 1979 I was designing and teaching design full time. All along Manry and *Tinkerbelle* lurked in the back of my mind and served as an inspiration, a way to pull everything together and give my life a focus.

In 1980 I sold my twenty-eight-foot trimaran and put all of my resources into the creation of *Napoleon Solo,* a small cruiser. I relied on a great deal of aid from my ex-wife, Frisha Hugessen, my good friend Chris Latchem, and a host of others. The design was unusual, though not at all radical. We took pains to create a handsome, meticulously constructed cold-molded craft, excellent in light airs and well-balanced and forgiving in heavy weather. *Solo* became much more than a boat to me. I knew her every nail and screw, every grain of wood. It was as if I'd created a living being. Sailors tend to feel that way about their boats. Chris and I gave *Solo* a harsh thousand-mile shakedown cruise from Annapolis to Massachusetts through late-fall gales. By the spring of 1981, I was ready to follow in Manry's wake.

I was not interested in setting a record as Manry had done. *Solo* was just over twenty-one feet long. There weren't many boats of her size that had made the crossing, but there had been a few as small as twelve feet. For me the crossing was more of an inner voyage and a pilgrimage, of sorts. It would also serve as a measuring stick for my competence as a seaman, a designer, and a craftsman. I figured that if I made it to England safely, I'd have accomplished every major goal I'd ever set for myself. From England I would continue south and west, measuring *Solo*'s performance in a single-handed transatlantic race called the Mini-Transat. That would carry me to Antigua. In the spring I would return to New England, thereby completing a circumnavigation of the North Atlantic. To qualify for the Mini-Transat, I had to sail six hundred miles alone in *Solo,* so I entered the Bermuda 1-2 Race and sailed from Newport to Bermuda. From there I would make the crossing to England with Chris.

When I departed the United States, it was with everything I owned, except for some tools. Few insurance brokers had wanted to talk to me, and those who did set such exorbitant premiums that it would cost less to buy materials for a second boat. I decided to take the risk. I told people that the worst that could happen was that I'd be killed, in which case I wouldn't be worried about collecting any insurance money. The second worst thing would be to lose *Solo.* It would take a while to recover, but I would. I knew plenty of other people who had lost their boats and recovered.

Many of my friends still couldn't understand why I wanted to undertake such a voyage, why I couldn't test myself without crossing the Atlantic. But there was more to the crossing than simply putting myself to the test. From the first time I ventured from the shore in a boat, I felt that my spirit was touched. On my first offshore trip to Bermuda, I began to think of the sea as my chapel. It was my soul that called me to this pilgrimage.

One friend suggested I write down my thoughts for the benefit of those who thought I was mad. While waiting for Chris in Bermuda, I sat beneath a palm tree and wrote the following: "I wish I could describe the feeling of being at sea, the anguish, frustration, and fear, the beauty that accompanies threatening spectacles, the spiritual communion with creatures in whose domain I sail. There is a magnificent intensity in life that comes when we are not in control but are only reacting, living, surviving. I am not a religious man per se. My own cosmology is convoluted and not in line with any particular church or philosophy. But for me, to go to sea is to get a glimpse of the face of God. At sea I am reminded of my insignificance—of all men's insignificance. It is a wonderful feeling to be so humbled."

The Atlantic crossing to England with Chris was exhilarating—gales, fast runs, whales, dolphins. It was the stuff adventure is made of. And as we approached the coast of England, I felt I was ending the whole experience that had begun at my birth, and beginning a new one.

ADRIFT

SEVENTY-SIX DAYS LOST AT SEA

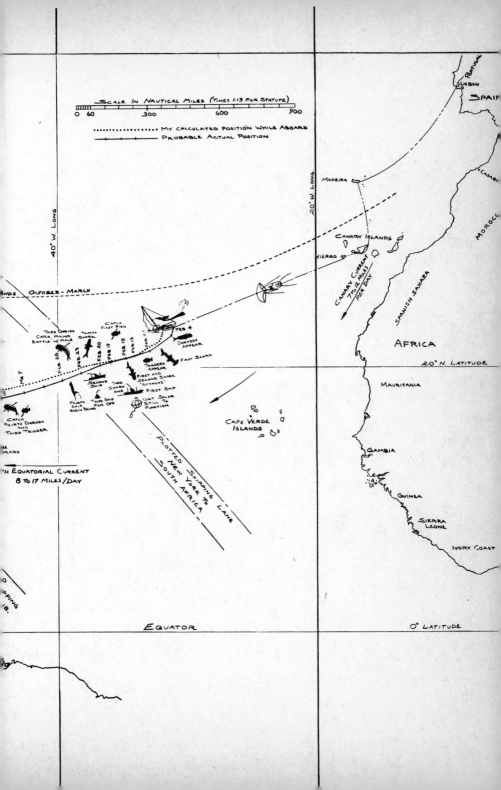

SCALE IN NAUTICAL MILES (TIMES 1.13 FOR STATUTE)

0 60   300   600   900

············ MY CALCULATED POSITION WHILE ABOARD
——┼—————┼—— PROBABLE ACTUAL POSITION

40° W LONG

20° W LONG

PORTUGAL
LISBON
SPAIN

MADEIRA

CASABL

MOROCC

CANARY ISLANDS

HIERRO

OCTOBER — MARCH

CANARY CURRENT
7 TO 12 MILES
PER DAY

SPANISH SAHARA

AFRICA

20° N. LATITUDE

MAURITANIA

THIRD DORADO
CATCH, MAJOR
BATTLE W/ MALE

CATCH
FIRST FISH

FEB 4

FOURTH
SHARK

DORADOS
APPEAR

FIRST SHARK

TRIGGERS
APPEAR

SECOND
SHIP

THIRD
SHARK AND

FIRST AND
SECOND SHARK
"ATTACKS"

FIRST SHIP

GAMBIA

FOURTH
SHIP
NORTH BOUND

THIRD SHIP
FAR OFF

GET SOLAR
STILL TO
FUNCTION

GUINEA

CATCH
FOURTH DORADO
AND
THIRD TRIGGER

CAPE VERDE
ISLANDS

SIERRA
LEONE

EQUATORIAL CURRENT
8 TO 17 MILES/DAY

PLOTTED SHIPPING LANE
NEW YORK TO
SOUTH AFRICA

IVORY COAST

PPING
B.

EQUATOR

0° LATITUDE

LOG
OF
NAPOLEON
SOLO

IT IS LATE at night. The fog has been dense for days. *Napoleon Solo* continues to slice purposefully through the sea toward the coast of England. We should be getting very close to the Scilly Isles. We must be very careful. The tides are large, the currents strong, and these shipping lanes heavily traveled. Both Chris and I are keeping a sharp eye out. Suddenly the lighthouse looms on the rocky isles, its beam high off the water. Immediately we see breakers. We're too close. Chris pushes the helm down and I trim the sails so that *Solo* sails parallel to the rocks that we can see. We time the change in bearing of the lighthouse to calculate our distance away—less than a mile. The light is charted to have a thirty-mile range. We are fortunate because the fog is not as thick as it often is back in our home waters of Maine. No wonder that in the single month of November 1893 no fewer than 298 ships scattered their bones among these rocks.

The next morning, *Solo* eases herself out of the white fog and over the swells in a light breeze. She slowly slips into the bay in which Penzance is nestled. The sea pounds against the granite cliffs of Cornwall on the southwest coast of England, which has claimed its own vast share of ships and lives. The jaws of the bay hold many dangers, such as the pile of rocks known as the Lizard.

Today the sky is bright and sunny. The sea is gentle. Green fields cap the cliffs. After our two-week passage from the Azores with only the smell of salt water in our lungs, the scent of land is sweet. At the end of every passage, I feel as if I am living the last page of a fairy tale, but this time the feeling is especially strong. Chris, who is my only crew, wings out the jib. It gently floats out over the water and tugs us past the village of Mousehole, which is perched in a crevice in the cliffs. We soon glide up to the high stone breakwater at Penzance and secure *Na-*

poleon Solo to it. With the final neat turns of docking lines around the cleats, we conclude *Solo's* Atlantic crossing and the last of the goals that I began setting for myself fifteen years ago. It was then that Robert Manry showed me not only how to dream, but also how to fulfill that dream. Manry had done it in a tiny boat called *Tinkerbelle*. I did it in *Solo*.

Chris and I climb up the stone quay to look for customs and the nearest pub. I look down on *Solo* and think of how she is a reflection of myself. I conceived her, created her, and sailed her. Everything I have is within her. Together we have ended this chapter of my life. It is time to dream new dreams.

Chris will soon depart and leave me to continue my journey with *Solo* alone. I've entered the Mini-Transat Race, which is a singlehanded affair. I don't need to think about that for a while. Now it is time for celebration. We head off to find a pint, the first we've had in weeks.

The Mini-Transat runs from Penzance to the Canaries and then on to Antigua. I want to go to the Caribbean anyway. Figure I'll find work there for the winter. *Solo* is a fast-cruising boat, and I'm interested to see how she fares against the spartan racers. I think I have a shot at finishing in the money since my boat is so well prepped. Some of my opponents are putting in bulkheads and drawing numbers on sails with Magic Markers in frantic pandemonium before the start. I indulge in local pasties and fish and chips. My last-minute jobs consist of licking stamps and sampling the local brew.

It is not all fun and games. It is the autumn equinox, when storms rage, and within a week two severe gales rip up the English Channel. Ships are cracked in half and many of the Transat competitors are delayed. One French boat capsizes and her crew can't right her. They take to their life raft and manage to land on a lonesome, tiny beach along a stretch of treacherous cliffs on the Brittany coast. Another Frenchman is not so lucky. His body and the transom of his boat are found crumpled on the Lizard. A black mood hangs over the fleet.

I make my way up to the local chandlery for final preparations. It is nestled in a mossy alleyway, and no sign marks its location. No one needs to post the way to old Willoughby's domain. I was warned that he talks a tough line, but in my few visits I have warmed up to his cynicism. Willoughby is squat, his legs bowed as if they have been steam-bent around a beer barrel, causing him to walk on the sides of his shoes. He slowly hobbles about the shop, weaving back and forth like an uncanvased ship in a swell. Beneath a gray tousle of hair, his eyes are squinted and sparkly. A pipe is clamped between his teeth.

Turning to one of his clerks, he motions toward the harbor. "All those little boats and crazy youngsters down there, nothin' but lots of work and headaches, I can tell you." Turning back to me he mutters, "Here to steal more bosunry from an old man and make him work like the devil to boot, I bet."

"That's right, no rest for the wicked," I tell him.

Willoughby raises a brow and twirks the faintest wrinkle of a grin, which he tries to hide behind his pipe. In no time he is spinning yarns big enough to knit the world a sweater. He ran away to sea at fifteen, served on square-riggers in the wool trade from Australia to England. He's been round Cape Horn so many times he's lost count.

"I heard about that Frenchman. Why you fellas go to sea for pleasure is beyond me. 'Course we had some fine times in my day, real fine times we had. But that was our stock in trade. A fella who'd go to sea for pleasure'd sure go to hell for a pastime."

I can tell the old man has a big space in his heart for all nautical lunatics, especially the young ones. "At least you'd have somebody to keep you company then, Mr. Willoughby."

"It's a bad business I tell you, a bad business," he says more seriously. "Sorry thing, that Frenchman. What do you get if you win this here race? Big prize?"

"No, I don't know really. Maybe a plastic cup or something."

"Ha! A fine state of affairs! You go out, play tag with Neptune, have a good chance to end up in old Davy Jones' locker—and for a cup. It's a good joke." And it is, too. The Frenchman has really affected the old man. He cheerily insists on slipping a few goodies onto my pile, free of charge, but his tone is somber. "Now don't come back and bother me any more."

"Next time I'm in town you can bet on me like the plague, or the tax man. Cheers!"

A little bell jingles laughingly as I close the door. I can hear Willoughby inside pacing to and fro on the creaking wooden floor. "A bad business, I tell you. It's a bad business."

The morning of the race's start, I make my way past the milling crowds to the skipper's meeting. Whether the race will start on time or not has been a matter of speculation for days. The last couple of gales that swept through had edged up to hurricane force. "Expect heavy winds at the start," a meteorologist tells us. "By nightfall they'll be up to force eight or so."

The crowd murmurs. "Starting in a bloody gale . . . Quiet, he's not finished yet."

"If you can weather Finisterre you'll be okay, but try to get plenty of sea room. Within thirty-six hours, all hell is going to break loose, with a good chance of force ten to twelve and forty-foot waves."

"Lovely," I say. "Anybody want to charter a small racing boat—cheap?" The crowd's talk grows loud. Heated debate breaks out between the racers and their supporters. Isn't it lunacy to start a transatlantic race in these conditions? The talk subsides as the race organizer breaks in.

"Please! Look, if we postpone we might not get off at all. It's late in the year and we could get locked in for weeks. We all knew it would probably be tough going to the Canaries. If you can get past Finisterre, you'll be home free. So keep in touch, stay awake, and good sailing."

The quay around Penzance's inner harbor is packed with people gawking and snapping pictures, waving, weeping or laughing. They will soon return to the comfort of their warm little houses.

NAPOLEON SOLO

I yell "Cheerio!" as *Solo* is towed out between the massive steel gates, which are opened by the harbormaster and his men pacing round an antique capstan. *Solo* and I are as prepared as we can be. My apprehension gives way to high spirits and excitement. The seconds tick by. My fellow racers and I maneuver about the starting line, making practice runs at it, adjusting our sails, shaking our arms to get the butterflies out of our stomachs. Those prone to seasickness will have a hard time. Warning colors go up. Get ready. Waves sweep into the bay; the wind is already growing, a rancorous circus sky flies in from the west. I reign *Solo* in, tack her over. Smoke puffs from the starting gun; its blast is blown away in the wind before it reaches my ears. *Solo* cuts across the line leading the fleet into the race.

At night the wind is stiff and the fleet fights hard against rising seas. I can often see the lights of the other boats, but by morning I see none. The bad conditions have abated. *Solo* slices quickly over the large, smooth swell. I spot a white triangle ahead, rising up and then disappearing behind the waves. I shake the reef out of the jib and one of the reefs out of the mains'l. *Solo* races on to catch the other boat. In a few hours I can see the white hull. It is an aluminum boat that was rafted next to me in Penzance, sailed by one of the two Italians in the race. Like most of the competitors, he's a friendly guy. Something seems slightly wrong. The foot of his jib, which has been reefed, is flogging around and bangs on the deck. I yell across, but get no response. I film the boat as I pass, then go below and radio him several times. No answer. Perhaps he's asleep. As night falls, I hear one of the other racers talking to the organizer on the radio. The Italian has sunk. Luckily he has been picked up. When I rode by him, he was probably in trouble and trying to keep the leak contained.

On the third day, I see a freighter pass about a mile away. I radio to him and learn that he has seen twenty-two of the twenty-six boats in the fleet behind me. I'm greatly encouraged. The wind grows. *Solo* beats into stiff seas. I must make a choice, either to risk being pushed into the notorious Bay of Biscay and try to squeak past Finisterre, or to tack and head out to sea. I choose the bay, hoping for the front to pass and to give me a lift so I can clear the cape. But the wind continues to increase, and soon *Solo* is leaping over ten-foot waves, pausing in midair for a second, and then crashing down on the other side. I have to hold on to keep from being thrown off of my seat. Wind screams through the rigging. For hours *Solo* weaves and slips sideways, shaking at every punch. Inside, the noise of the sea pounding against the hull is deafening. Pots and cans clatter. An oil bottle shatters. After eight hours of it, I adjust. It is dark. There is nothing to do but push on. I crawl aft into my cabin, which is a little quieter than forward, wedge myself into my bunk, and go to sleep.

When I awake, my foul-weather gear is floating about in a pool of water. I leap through the pool and find a crack in the hull. With every passing wave, water shoots in and the crack grows longer. The destruction of *Solo* would follow like falling dominoes. As quick as a mongoose, I rip down the sails, cut lumber, and shore her up. For two days I guide her slowly to the coast of Spain.

Within twenty-four hours of my arrival in La Coruña, seven Mini-Transat boats arrive. Two have been hit by cargo ships, one has broken a rudder, others are fed up. It appears that *Solo* ran into some floating debris. Her hull is streaked with dents. Perhaps it was a log. I've seen plenty of them—even whole trees adrift. Over the years I've spoken with voyagers who have sighted everything from truck containers that fell off of ships to spiky steel balls that resembled World War II mines. One boat off the coast of the United States even found a rocket!

The race is finished for me. I speak no Spanish, so it is difficult to organize repairs. I can't find a Frenchman who will agree to drive over the rocky and pitted Spanish roads to retrieve *Solo*. I have little money. My boat is full of seawater, spilled cooking oil, and broken glass. My electronic self-steering is fried.

Then I become ill, with a fever of 103°. I lie among the soggy mess, thoroughly depressed.

Still, I am more fortunate than others. Out of the twenty-five boats that started, no fewer than five have been totally lost, although luckily no one has drowned. Only half of the fleet will reach the finish in Antigua.

It is four weeks before I complete my repairs and put *Napoleon Solo* to sea again. I don't know if I have enough stores and money to reach the Caribbean, but I don't have enough to go home. Luckily the Club Nautico de La Coruña is kind. "No charge. We do what we can for the man alone." For four weeks gales daily ravage Finisterre. The harbor is full of crews waiting to escape to the south. We are all just a little late in the season. In the morning there is frost on the deck. Each day it remains longer before melting off. When *Solo* finally claws past Finisterre, I feel as though I've passed Cape Horn.

I've picked up one person to crew, a Frenchwoman named Catherine Pouzet. I needed someone to steer. Catherine's only previous ocean experience was on a boat that was dismasted in the Bay of Biscay. In a panic they had radioed for assistance, were picked up by a tanker, and had watched their boat—the dream they'd worked years for—drift away. They had operated under the delusion that the tanker would save their boat, too. Catherine was not easily put off. She "auto-stopped" her way to La Coruña and there tried yacht-stopping for a ride south.

Catherine loves my little boat, and she is lovely herself, but I feel no desire for romance. I want only for past pain to melt away in the sun of the south. With Catherine's help, I expect to reach the Canaries in fourteen days.

For four weeks we crawl south to Lisbon. Between zephyrs we flop about on a mirrored sea. In my reflection in the glassy water, I get a hint that I am going nowhere, but I begin to fall into the slow pace of the cruising life. My disappointment at not completing the Mini-Transat begins to fade.

On the coast of Spain, ancient river valleys cut deeply into the country. In these rugged *rías,* modern machinery consists of donkeys pulling ox carts with wooden wheels and axles. Peasants collect animal bedding from the uncultured grasses of mountainside clearings. Women gather at community basins to beat clothes clean on rocks or concrete. In one port the officials pore over our entry forms, carrying them from office to office, like children trying to decipher hieroglyphics. We are the first yacht to anchor in their waters in over a year.

We proceed along the coast into Portugal, cutting through dense fog and dodging freighters, which on a clear night appear like strings of Christmas tree lights, sixteen or seventeen visible at any time. To one side of us is a coast of rocky teeth and seething seas, on the other the *drum, drum* of heavy engines. When the sails hang lifeless, we row. Often we make only ten miles a day.

It would have been simple to remain at anchor. Latin life and lazy weather are drugging. We begin to soak up tranquility like a sponge. Among the cruising community we make many friends traveling in the same general direction. Many are French. All planned to be into the Pacific by January, but their plans have been tempered. "Maybe we'll hole up in Gibraltar for the winter." But there is something inside of me itching to push on. It is more than the need to get to a place where I can refill my purse. Catherine sometimes pouts, wishing I would open up to her more. "You are a hard man," she tells me, but I do not respond by becoming softer. I only become more resolved to reach the Canaries and then push on alone.

We sail from Lisbon in decent wind and reach the peaks of Madeira, pause there, and then proceed south to Tenerife. Our two-week voyage has taken six. I say good-by to Catherine. My ship and I are at peace with one another once again.

Solo is well received wherever she goes. The local people, who would often steer clear of big, expensive yachts, flock to *Solo* like bears to honey. She is as small as their open coastal fishing boats. It is unbelievable to them that she has come all the way from America. In one small port, all of the fishermen and boatbuilders come down early each morning and perch along the quay, patiently waiting for me to wake up. They are eager for me to tell them more stories in my broken Spanish and convoluted sign language.

I come very close to mooring *Solo* for a winter. It has happened to many others, sailing in for a week's visit and staying for years. They make ends meet by making ships in bottles or collecting pine cones in the mountains. German tourists cover the beaches and buy anything with a For Sale sign. I might draw pictures, and I have some writing to do.

I need more than just looking on, playing tourist. I need to be productive, to create, and, of course, to earn money again since I have only a few dollars left and debts to repay.

I am caught in the sailor's inevitable dilemma. When you are at sea you know you must reach harbor, to restock and, you hope, rest in a warm caress. You need ports and often can't wait to get to the next. Then when you are in port, you can't wait to get back to sea again. After a few glasses of cold beer and a few nights in a dry bed, the ocean calls, and you follow her. You need mother earth, but you love the sea.

In most ports you can find a crew who wants to go in the same direction you do. But now most people who wanted to get to the Caribbean for the winter have left some time ago. I don't think that the trip will be difficult alone. One of my newfound friends on Tenerife has repaired my self-steering gear, and the pilot chart promises that there is only a 2 percent chance of encountering gales. The trade winds should be steady. It'll be a milk run.

I make my way to the sparsely populated island of Hierro. Steep cliffs rise from the Atlantic to the east, topped by lush hills and green valleys. The island slopes away to the west and ends with a moonscape of small volcanoes, rocky rubble, and hot red sand. I finish stocking in a tiny man-made port on the western end. On the final day my throat is dry and gravelly. I slap my last pesetas down on the bar. In fumbling Spanish I tell the familiar bartender that the coins will do me no good at sea. *"Cerveza, por favor!"* The beer is cold. The bartender sits down beside me.

"Where to?"

"Caribbean. Work. No more pesetas."

He nods, contemplating the length of the voyage. "Such a small boat. No problema?"

"Pequeño barco, pequeño problema. No big problem yet, anyway!" We laugh and talk while I finish my beer, bum a last cigarette, sling my provisions over my shoulder, and head for the quay.

One of the old fishermen stops me. "You come from America?" he asks as he slits open part of his catch, cleans it, and flops it onto a scale. A woman dressed in black pokes the fish, chattering away to herself.

"Yes, America." I wonder if her man was a fisherman lost at sea, like so many others.

"Ooh ho!" he says. "In such a small boat? *Tonto!"* Fool.

"It's not so small, it's my whole house."

The old man gestures toward his lower abdomen with cupped hands as if holding gigantic organs. We laugh at his joke as I shake my head no, open my eyes wide, and shiver as if frightened. The woman grabs him by the arm, obviously telling him the fish is overpriced, and begins bargaining, an ageless custom as ritualized as the dominoes played by the men seated at a folding card table on the stony beach.

The night of January 29 is clear, the sky peppered with bright stars. Blocks squeak as I pull up the sails and glide out of the harbor. I thread my way through the offshore fishing fleet and point *Solo* toward the Caribbean. It feels good to be at sea again.

NERVES
EXPOSED

〰〰〰〰〰〰 I AM EXPERIENCING
a rare time for a sailor, a week of peace. With uncharacteristic
gentleness, the sea and wind wrap my boat in a motherly caress
that sends her skipping toward Antigua. I am comforted by the
sea yet am continually awed by her. Like an old friend she is
always familiar, yet she is always changing and full of surprises.
I recline on the afterdeck and feel the regular files of waves
approach, lift my ship three or four feet as they roll under her,
then ease her down gently as they rush on, slipping into the
horizon ahead. The breeze rustles the pages of my novel while
the sun browns my skin and bleaches my hair.

An age ago oceanic greyhounds—great clipper ships, whalers,
and fast cutters full of slaves—plied this route from the Canaries to the Caribbean. Trade winds filled the cloudlike sails
that hung from their towering spars: stuns'ls, tops'ls, royals, all
set. The rattling of *Solo*'s spars and the hum of her auto pilot
mix with the running wind and blow into my ears a fantasy of
tapping feet in a hornpipe danced to the song of a concertina.

Solo smoothly cuts westward with twin jibs spread from her
bow. Her bubbling trail curls across the waves astern. When
not reading, I scratch out stories and letters, scribble pictures
of sea serpents with bow ties, and waste inordinate amounts of
film, shooting the sea, boat maneuvers, sunsets. I stuff myself
with fried potatoes, onions, eggs, cheese, and grains—bulgur,
rolled oats, millet. I exercise—pushups, pullups, and yoga—
thrusting, twisting, and stretching in rhythm with the rolling
boat. A spidery, animated maze of mast, boom, struts, and poles
dips, rises, and spreads the sails to catch the wind. In short, I
and my ship are in fine shape, and I am having a wonderful and
leisurely sail. If good fortune continues, I will reach my destination before February 25.

On February 4 the wind rises and begins to whistle through

the rigging. A gale begins to sweep in. A blanket of clouds races overhead. Seas build and begin to crash down all around us. I want to return to peaceful sailing. I speak to the sky. "Come on, hit me if you must, and then go quickly."

My little boat continues to slice across undulating foothills that are rapidly growing into small mountains. The water that was sparkling clear now reflects the dark, threatening sky. Waves froth and spit at us as we carve around them toward the sinking sun. *Solo* is kept more or less on course by the electric automatic pilot. Its motor hums a fatiguing song as it constantly works overtime. Despite the occasional waterfalls that cascade across the deck, I am not too uncomfortable. I joke in front of my movie camera, gnaw on a greasy sausage, and belch in a Long John Silver croak: "Aargh, matey, as you can see, we's havin' just fine weather. Course we could do with a bit o' wind." I crawl up on the foredeck and stuff one of the jibs into its sack. Cold water runs down my spine and up my arms.

The sky grows darker as dusk approaches. When *Solo* slides into the wave troughs, the sun dips to the horizon. Dip, dip, and it finally drowns in the west. *Solo* slashes on into the night. The waves and wind seem to grow fiercer at night. I cannot see the waves far off—and then suddenly they are here, breaking and rushing down on us. Then they scurry away again into the shadow of the world almost before I am aware that they have struck.

For over ten thousand miles and one and a half Atlantic crossings, my ship and I have kept each other company. She has seen worse, much worse. If things significantly deteriorate, I can adopt storm tactics: reduce sail, and either heave to or run downwind. The pilot chart promises infrequent gales of minor intensity for this part of the south Atlantic and time of year. The wind can pipe up to force seven or so, enough to muss one's hair and guarantee a bathing on deck, but not enough to loosen one's dentures. In about two weeks I will be lying in the baking sun of the Caribbean with a cold rum punch in hand.

Solo will be placidly anchored with sails furled beneath some palm-studded beach.

Fortunately I rarely have to be on deck; only to reef the sails or to change jibs. I have provided the boat with an inside steering and central control station. I sit beneath a Plexiglas hatch that looks like a boxy jet canopy. From here I can steer with an inside tiller, adjust the sails by reaching out through the open washboard to the cleats and winches beside the hatch, and keep watch, all at the same time. In addition, I can look at the chart on the table below me, chat on the radio beside me, or cook up a meal on the galley stove, all without leaving my seat. Despite the acrobatics of the sea, the cabin remains relatively comfortable. Save for an occasional drip of water feeling its way through the crevices of the hatch, my surroundings are dry. The air hangs heavy with the dampness of the coming storm, but the varnished wood of the cabin glows warmly in the soft light. The shapes contained in the wood grain become animals, people, companions. They calm me. The small amount of coffee that I manage to transfer from my lurching cup to my mouth warms me and props my eyes open. My stomach, made of some non-corroding, inexplodable, and otherwise nonimpressionable alloy, does not yearn for a dry biscuit diet; instead, I eat heartily and plan for my birthday dinner two days from now. I can't bake a cake, having no oven, but I will have a go at chocolate crêpes. I'll stir a tin of rabbit I've saved into a curry, ignoring the French superstition that even the slightest mention of *lapin* assures a crew the most wretched luck.

Though I feel secure in my floating nest, the storm reawakens my caution, which has slumbered for a week. Each ten-foot wave that sweeps by contains more tons of water than I care to imagine. The wind whistles across the deck and through the rigging wires. Occasionally *Solo*'s rear is kicked, and she brings her head to wind as if to see the striking bully. The jib luffs with a rustling rattle, then pulls taut as *Solo* turns off to continue on her way. Visions of a rogue wave snap into my mind. Caused by the coincidence of peaks traveling in different directions or at different speeds, a rogue can grow to four times the average wave height and could throw *Solo* about like a toy. Converging wave troughs can also form a canyon into which we could plunge. Often such anomalies flow from different directions, forming vertical cliffs from which seas tumble in liquid avalanches.

Six months ago *Solo* fell with a thunderous bang in just such a cascade off the Azores. The sky disappeared and nothing but green was visible across the deck hatch. The boat immediately righted and we sailed on, but it was a hard knock. My books and sextant leaped over the tall fiddle rails, smashing on the chart table and splintering its moldings. If they had not hit the table, they would have landed in my face. I was lucky that time; I must be more cautious.

Disaster at sea can happen in a moment, without warning, or it can come after long days of anticipation and fear. It does not always come when the sea is fiercest but may spring when waters lie as flat and imperturbable as a sheet of iron. Sailors may be struck down at any time, in calm or in storm, but the sea does not do it for hate or spite. She has no wrath to vent. Nor does she have a hand of kindness to extend. She is merely there, immense, powerful, and indifferent. I do not resent her indifference, or my comparative insignificance. Indeed, it is one of the main reasons I like to sail: the sea makes the insignificance of my own small self and of all humanity so poignant.

I watch *Solo's* boiling, phosphorescent wake as it dissipates among the somersaulting waves. "Things could be worse," I muse. Then voices from the past speak to me. "Each time you have chanted that phrase, things have inevitably gotten worse." I think of the pilot chart figures, which are averages taken from ships' data. There might be some truth to the idea that charted estimates of gale strengths tend to be low. After all, if a captain hears of bad weather, he doesn't usually head his rust bucket for the center of it in order to get some fresh air. No doubt I will be a bit uncomfortable for a few days.

I check my gear over and make sure all is as secure and shipshape as a floating fool can make it. I inspect the hull, deck, bulkheads, cabinetry, and all of the joints that hold my wooden jewelry box secure. The kettle is filled for coffee or steaming lemonade. A lump of chocolate is at hand beside the radio. All essential preparations have been made.

It is about 22:30 Greenwich Mean Time. The moon hangs full, white and motionless, undisturbed by the tempest and the tumultuous sea. If conditions continue to worsen, I will have to head more southerly. For the time being, I can do nothing more, so I lie down to rest. At 23:00 I get up and undress. I lie down again clothed only in a T-shirt. A watch circles my wrist, and around my neck is a slab of whale tooth on a string. It is the most I will wear the next two and a half months.

My boat slues around the rushing peaks, her keel clinging to the slopes like a mountain goat, her port side pressed down against the black, rolling ocean. I lie on my bunk, slung upon the lee canvas, hanging as if in a hammock.

BANG! A deafening explosion blankets the subtler sounds of torn wood fiber and rush of sea. I jump up. Water thunders over me as if I've suddenly been thrown into the path of a rampaging river. Forward, aft— where does it come from? Is half of the side gone? No time. I fumble with the knife I have sheathed by the chart table. Already the water is waist deep. The nose of the boat is dipping down. *Solo* comes to a halt as she begins a sickening dive. She's going down, down! My mind barks orders. Free the emergency package. My soul screams. You've lost her! I hold my breath, submerge, slash at the tie-downs that secure my emergency duffel. My heart is a pounding pile driver. The heavy work wrings the air from my lungs and my mind battles with my limbs for the opportunity to breathe. Terminal darkness and chaos surround me. Get out, get out, she's going down! In one rhythmic movement I rocket upward, thrust the hatch forward, and catapult my shaking body onto the deck, leaving my package of hope behind.

Less than thirty seconds have elapsed since impact. The bow points toward its grave at a hesitating low angle and the sea washes about my ankles. I cut the tie-downs that secure the raft canister. Thoughts flash about me like echoes in a cave. Perhaps I have waited too long. Perhaps it is time to die. Going down . . . die . . . lost without trace. I recall the life raft instructions: throw the bulky hundred pounds overboard before inflation. Who can maneuver such weight in the middle of a bucking circus ride? No time, quickly—she's going down! I yank. The first pull, then the second—nothing, nothing! This is it, the end of my life. Soon, it will come soon. I scream at the stubborn canister. "Come on, you bastard!" The third pull comes up hard, and she blows with a bursting static *shush*. A wave sweeps over the entire deck, and I simply float the raft off. It thrashes about on the end of its painter. *Solo* has been transformed from a proper little ship to a submerged wreck in about one minute. I dive into the raft with the knife clenched in my teeth, buccaneer style, noticing that the movie camera mounted on the aft pulpit has been turned on. Its red eye winks at me. Who is directing this film? He isn't much on lighting but his flair for the dramatic is impressive.

Unmoving and unconcerned, the moon looks down upon us. Its lunar face is eclipsed by wisps of clouds that waft across it, dimming the shadow of *Solo*'s death. My instincts and training have carried me through the motions of survival, but now, as I have a moment to reflect, the full impact of the crash throbs in my head. Never have all of my senses seemed so sharp. My emotions are an incomprehensible mix. There is a wailing anguish that mourns the loss of my boat. There is a deep disappointment in myself for my failures. Overshadowing it all is the stark realization that what I think and feel will not matter much longer. My body shakes with cold. I am too far from civilization to have any hope of rescue.

In the space of a moment, myriad conversations and debates flash through my mind, as if a group of men are chattering within my skull. Some of them joke, finding comic relief in the camera's busily taking pictures that no one will ever see. Others stoke a furnace of fear. Fear becomes sustenance. Its energy feeds action. I must be careful. I fight blind panic: I do not want the power from my pumping adrenalin to lead to confused and counterproductive activity. I fight the urge to fall into catatonic hysteria: I do not want to sit frozen in fear until the end comes. Focus, I tell myself. Focus and get moving.

I see my vessel, my companion, my child, swallowed up like a crumb too small for the deep Atlantic to taste. Waves bury her and pass. *Solo's* white decks emerge. She's not going down, not yet. Wait until she goes before cutting the painter. Even though I have added canned water and other gear to the raft's supplies, I will not live long without additional equipment. Wait and salvage everything you can. My body shakes even more with fright and cold, and my eyes sting from the salt. I must get some clothes, some cover, anything. I begin hacking off a piece of the mains'l. Don't cut the raft, be careful, careful. Once cut, the sailcloth rips off easily. The raft flips about as I pull the horseshoe life preserver and man-overboard pole off of *Solo's* stern. Foam and sea continue to sweep across her, but she rises each time. My mind coaxes her. Please don't go, not yet, please stay up. The watertight compartments that I designed and installed have combined with pockets of air trapped inside of her. She fights back. Her jib snaps with loud report. Her hatch and rudder bang as the ocean beats her. Perhaps she will not sink after all. Her head is under but her rear hesitates like a child at the shore, unable to make the final plunge.

I ache with cold; the stench of rubber, plastic, and talc fill my nostrils. *Solo* may sink any moment now, but I must get back inside. There isn't much time. I pull up to the side of the boat, climb aboard, and stand for a second feeling the strange sensation of being in the sea and on deck at the same time. Waves rear up and bury the boat, but time after time *Solo* struggles to the surface. How much battering will she take before water feels its way into the few remaining air spaces? How many moments are left before she will disappear for the last time?

Between towering crests that wash over me, I lower myself into the hatch. The water below is peaceful compared to the surrounding tempest. I duck into the watery tomb, and the hatch slams shut behind me with a crack. I feel for the emergency bag and cut away the lines that secure it. Waves wander by, engulf us, and move on. I gasp for air. The bag is freed but seems to weigh as much as the collected sins of the world. While struggling in the companionway, pushing and tugging to get the gear on deck, I fight the hatch, which beats against my back. Heaving the bag into the raft requires all the strength I have.

As it tumbles into the raft, I turn to reenter the hatch. My hand turns aft and finds a piece of floating cushion wedged against the overhead. Jerking at it, I arise for a gulp of air. There is none. In that moment I feel as though the last breath in the galaxy has been breathed by someone else. The edge of the sea suddenly rips past. I see the surface shimmering like a thousand candles. Air splutters in, and I gasp as the clatter of *Solo* becomes muffled by the coming of the next wave.

I tie the cushion to the end of a halyard and let it float about while I submerge to retrieve my bed. Bundling up my wet sleeping bag is like capturing an armful of snakes. I slowly manage to shove, pull, and roll the bag into the raft. With the final piece of cushion, I fall in behind. I have successfully abandoned ship.

My God, *Solo* is still floating! I see her slowly rolling farther onto her side as I gather up items that float out of the cabin one by one: a cabbage, an empty Chock Full o' Nuts coffee can, and a box containing a few eggs. The eggs will probably not last long, but I take them anyway.

I am too exhausted to do any more. I will not part from *Solo*, but should she want to leave I must be able to let go. Seventy feet of ⅜-inch line, tied to the end of the mainsheet, allows me to drift well downwind. *Solo* disappears when we dip into the waves' troughs. Great foaming crests of water grind their way toward us. There is a churning up to windward like the surf on the shore. I hear it coming; I hear the clap and bang and snap that are *Solo*'s words to me, "I'm here." The raft rises to meet the head of the wave that rushes toward me. The froth and curl crash by just to port.

The entrance fly on the tent-type cover snaps with a ripping sound each time the Velcro seal is blown by the wind. I must turn the raft or a breaker may drive through the opening. While on a wave peak, I look aft at *Solo*'s deck mounting on the next swell. The sea rises smoothly from the dark, a giant sitting up after a sleep. There is a tight round opening in the opposite side of the tent. I stick myself through this observation port up to my waist. I must not let go of the rope to *Solo*, but I need to move it. I loop a rope through the mainsheet which trails from *Solo*'s deck and lead it back to the raft. One end of this I secure to the handline around the raft's perimeter. The other I wind around the handline and bring the tail through the observation port. If *Solo* sinks I can let go of this tail and we will slip apart. Wait—can't get back in . . . I'm stuck. I try to free myself from the canopy clutching my chest. The sea spits at me. Crests roar in the darkness. I twist and yank and fall back inside. The raft swings and presents the wall of the tent to the waves. Ha! A good joke, the wall of a tent against the sea, the sea that beats granite to sand.

With a slipknot I tie *Solo*'s line to the handhold webbing that encircles the inside of the raft. While frantically tying all of my equipment to the webbing, I hear rumbling well to windward. It must be a big wave to be heard so far off. I listen to its approach. A rush of water, then silence. I can feel it rising over me. There is a wrenching rubbery shriek from the raft as the wave bursts upon us and my space collapses in half. The windward side punches in and sends me flying across the raft. The top collapses and water shoots in everywhere. The impact is

$\approx$ 25

There is a wrenching rubbery shriek from the raft
as the wave bursts upon us.

strengthened by the jerking painter, tied to my ship full of water, upwind from where the sea sprang. I'm going to die. Tonight. Here some 450 miles away from the nearest land. The sea will crush me, capsize me, and rob my body of heat and breath. I will be lost, and no one will even know until I'm weeks overdue.

I crawl back to windward, keeping one hand on the cord to *Solo*, the other hand clutching the handline. I huddle in my sodden sleeping bag. Gallons of water slosh about in the bottom of the raft. I sit on the cushion, which insulates me from the icy floor. I'm shivering but begin to warm up. It is a time to wait, to listen, to think, to plan, and to fear.

As my raft and I rise to the crest of a wave, I can see *Solo* wallowing in the following trough. Then she rises against the face of the next wave as I plummet into the trough that had cradled her a moment before. She has rolled well over now, with her nose and starboard side under and her stern quarter fairly high. If only you will stay afloat until morning. I must see you again, must see the damage that I feel I have caused you. Why didn't I wait in the Canaries? Why didn't I soften up and relax? Why did I drive you to this so that I could complete my stupid goal of a double crossing? I'm sorry, my poor *Solo*.

I have swallowed a lot of salt and my throat is parched. Perhaps in the morning I can retrieve more gear, jugs of water, and some food. I plan every move and every priority. The loss of body heat is the most immediate danger, but the sleeping bag may give me enough protection. Water is the first priority, then food. After that, whatever else I can grab. Ten gallons of water rest in the galley locker just under the companionway—forty to eighty days' worth of survival rations waiting for me just a hundred feet away. The raised stern quarter will make it easier to get aft. There are two large duffels in the aft cabin, hung on the topsides; one is full of food—about a month's worth—and the other is full of clothes. If I can dive down and swim forward, I may be able to pull my survival suit out of the forepeak. I dream of how its thick neoprene will warm me up.

Waves continue to pound the raft, beating the side in, pouring in water. The tubes are as tight as teak logs, yet they are bent like spaghetti. Bailing with the coffee can again and again, I wonder how much one of these rafts can take and watch for signs of splitting.

A small overhead lamp lights my tiny new world. The memory of the crash, the rank odor of my surroundings, the pounding of the sea, the moaning wind, and my plan to reboard *Solo* in the morning roll over and over in my brain. Surely it will end soon.

I am lost about halfway between western Oshkosh and Nowhere City. I do not think the Atlantic has emptier waters. I am about 450 miles north of the Cape Verde Islands, but they stand across the wind. I can drift only in the direction she blows. Downwind, 450 miles separate me from the nearest shipping lanes. Caribbean islands are the closest possible landfall, eighteen hundred nautical miles away. Do not think of it. Plan for daylight, instead. I have hope if the raft lasts. Will it last? The sea continues to attack. It does not always give warning. Often the curl develops just before it strikes. The roar accompanies the crash, beating the raft, ripping at it.

FEBRUARY 5
DAY 1

I hear a growl a long way off, toward the heart of the storm. It builds like a crescendo, growing louder and louder until it consumes all of the air around me. The fist of Neptune strikes, and with its blast the raft is shot to a staggering halt. It squawks and screams, and then there is peace, as though we have passed into the realm of the afterlife where we cannot be further tortured.

Quickly I yank open the observation port and stick my head out. *Solo*'s jib is still snapping and her rudder clapping, but I am drifting away. Her electrics have fused together and the strobe light on the top of her mast blinks good-by to me. I watch for a long time as the flashes of light become visible less often, knowing it is the last I will see of her, feeling as if I have lost a friend and a part of myself. An occasional flash appears, and then nothing. She is lost in the raging sea.

I pull up the line that had tied me to my friend, my hope for food and water and clothing. The rope is in one piece. Perhaps the loop I had tied in the mainsheet broke during the last shock. Or the knot; perhaps it was the knot. The vibration and surging might have shaken it loose. Or I may have made a mistake in tying it. I have tied thousands of bowlines; it is a process as familiar as turning a key. Still . . . No matter now. No regrets. I simply wonder if this has saved me. Did my tiny rubber home escape just before it was torn to pieces? Will being set adrift kill me in the end?

Somewhat relieved from the constant assault on the raft, I chide myself in a Humphrey Bogart fashion. Well, you're on your own now, kid. Mingled with the relief is fright, pain, remorse, apprehension, hope, and hopelessness. My feelings are bundled up in a massive ball of inseparable confusion, devouring me as a black hole gobbles up light. I still ache with cold, and now my body is shot through with pain from wounds that I've not noticed before. I feel so vulnerable. There are no backup systems remaining, no place to bail out to, no more second chances. Mentally and physically, I feel as if all of the protection has been peeled away from my nerves and they lie completely exposed.

THE WITCH AND HER CURSE: HUNGER AND THIRST

slide up and down breaking waves throughout the night. I have set the sea anchor—a piece of cloth that acts like a parachute in the water, slowing our descent and preventing us from capsizing. A wave breaks under us and throws the raft up until it rests on its front edge like a top. Gallons of black brine flood the raft. As I dangle from the handlines, hammering crests batter me through the raft's thin bottom. Just before we make a complete flip, the sea anchor comes up taut and jerks the raft back down. Newly scooped seawater rushes back upon me like a cold spring stream.

My life raft is a standard Avon six-man model composed of two multisegmented inner tubes, one stacked on the other. The inside diameter is about five feet, six inches. Before the start of the Mini-Transat, the race committee inspected *Solo* and was surprised to find such a large raft. "Have you ever gotten into a four-man raft?" I asked them. I had. I once blew one up and two friends joined me inside. We were literally on top of one another, our knees overlapping. Survival for more than a few days, with the raft loaded to legal capacity, would be questionable, and torturous at best. I figured a six-man raft might suffice for a crew of two for a moderate to long-term voyage.

Spanning the top tube is a semicircular arch tube that supports the tentlike canopy. One quarter of the canopy is loose to form the entry opening. The only spot with full sitting headroom is directly in the center of the raft. I can wedge myself against the outside perimeter so my head pushes up into the canopy, or slouch down to brace myself across the bottom. The raft is constructed of black dacron-reinforced rubber material, which is glued together. Extra strips of this material are laid over the seams. I'm only too aware of the many cases where life rafts have been torn apart. I memorize each cobweb of glue where

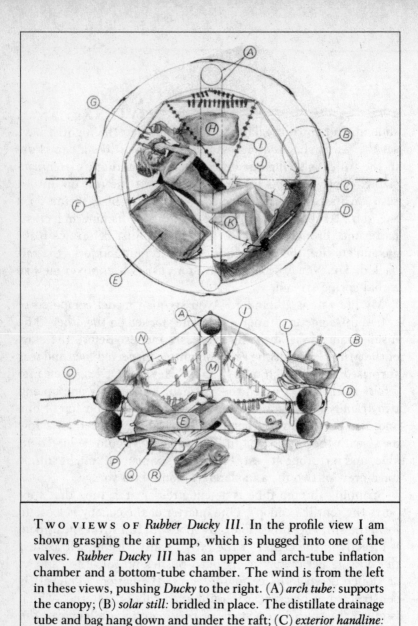

TWO VIEWS OF *Rubber Ducky III*. In the profile view I am shown grasping the air pump, which is plugged into one of the valves. *Rubber Ducky III* has an upper and arch-tube inflation chamber and a bottom-tube chamber. The wind is from the left in these views, pushing *Ducky* to the right. (A) *arch tube*: supports the canopy; (B) *solar still*: bridled in place. The distillate drainage tube and bag hang down and under the raft; (C) *exterior handline*: runs all around the outside of the raft; (D) *spray skirt or bib*:

across the entry opening, keeps some waves out and provides a shelf for the spear gun; (E) *equipment bag:* salvaged from *Solo,* contains the bulk of gear; (F) *cushion:* made of two-inch-thick closed-cell foam, which does not absorb water. This helps to cushion blows from sharks and fish under the raft; (G) *interior handline:* serves as an anchor for all the equipment. Fish are strung up between the anchor points. In the plan view the arrow points to the water bottle, sheath knife, and short pieces of line in position for instantaneous access; (H) *raft equipment bag:* supplied with the raft when purchased. It contains standard equipment such as the air pump and it is secured to an anchor point on the floor; (I) *clothesline:* to hang fish in the "butcher shop." Strung between the handline anchor points and up to the canopy arch tube; (J) *entry opening* (shown by the phantom line): kept on the forward right quarter of the raft away from the wind and approaching waves; (K) *sail cloth:* salvaged from *Solo,* folded and tied. Helps to cushion fish blows and to protect the raft from damage from the spear tip when fish are landed; (L) *Tupperware box:* wedged in the solar still bridle where it catches rain. Later on it will be positioned on the top of the canopy arch tube on its own bridle, and then inside under the leaky observation port; (M) *EPIRB* (Emergency Position-Indicating Radio Beacon): sends a signal on two frequencies monitored by commercial flights; (N) *observation port:* leaks badly and must be tied up since it is on the windward side. Eventually a water collection cape will drain through this opening into the Tupperware container; (O) *painter to the man-overboard pole:* trails astern, and serves as speedometer. It also keeps the raft aligned properly and prevents capsize. The pole increases my visibility. The line gives a good surface for the growth of barnacles, on which I and the triggerfish feed; (P) *gas cylinder:* inflated *Rubber Ducky.* Its vulnerable position is always a worry; (Q) *ballast pocket:* four pockets on the bottom fill with water to prevent capsizes; (R) *sagging floor:* typical where any weight pushes down. Water pressure otherwise forces the floor to arch upward slightly. The bumps pushing downward make good targets for fish, such as the dorado shown aiming for my left foot.

the tubes join and continually watch for any sign of tearing or stretching. The top and arch tube make up one inflation chamber and the bottom tube another. The safety valves spill any pressure in excess of two and one-half pounds per square inch. It is impossible to inflate the tubes by mouth; an air pump must be used. The entire structure is constantly undulating like an uneasy, coiled snake.

The thin rubber floor ripples and rolls, as if it were a waterbed being jumped upon by two sizable kangaroos. Kneeling, I hang on with one hand while using the coffee can to bail with the other. The floor sags around my knees. Bilge-water rivers run toward the sags; I intercept them with the can. Each time I finish there is another convulsion, another flooding of my cave, and the whole process begins again. The work is warming but fatiguing. There is no rest. The continual motion and the stench of rubber, glue, and talc from the new raft nauseate me, but I am too exhausted to throw up.

The ocean persists, monotonously bombarding us. Please don't knock us over; I can't survive a capsize. If I am thrown into the sea I will shiver until the earth quakes. My lips will turn blue, my skin white. My grasp will loosen. The sea will fold her blanket over me for one last time, and I will sleep forever. So I keep my weight and my gear on the side of the attack to aid stability, grasp the handline tight, and listen. My face feels permanently carved into a worried frown. In the dark I imagine a skullish face without comfort or compassion staring into my own. The sounds of the sea are like gun blasts, and I drift in and out of semiconscious dreams of war.

Finally blackness yields to gray. Colors begin to blossom. Morning sun sneaks into my dungeon and brings me a glimmer of hope. I have survived the night. The coming of day has never meant so much; but the gale rages on. I've often experienced gales at sea, but belowdecks there has always been a separation, if slight, from the storm. This tempest rages within

FEBRUARY 5
DAY 1

the raft as well as out. The flapping of the wind-beaten tent accompanies the ripping of the useless Velcro seal and the rattling of the entry closure. Water spews through the air. I sit in a submerged sponge, as the raft bounces its way across the heaving Atlantic.

Should I turn on the Emergency Position-Indicating Radio Beacon? The EPIRB has a range of 250 miles. It is rated to operate for seventy-two hours. Then the range will decrease until the battery dies. A commercial airline can hear its silent cry for help and send a search plane to home in on the radio beam. Ships in the vicinity are then notified. I *will* be saved.

Who am I kidding? I'm 800 miles west of the Canaries, 450 miles north of the Cape Verde Islands, and some 450 miles east of the nearest major shipping lane. Flights to the islands probably come by way of Europe and Africa. I had never seen a plane traveling to or from the Canaries across my current position. My chart shows no major African city that would attract intercontinental air traffic anywhere within 450 miles. There is no one to hear me.

I flip on the EPIRB switch anyway . . . just in case I'm wrong. I hope I'm wrong. Recently, a trimaran named *Boatfile* capsized and sank. The life raft was torn to pieces, leaving the crew bobbing in the open Atlantic in nothing but their survival suits. But the EPIRB that they hung on to brought help in a matter of hours. Two men in an immense and tossing sea were found and picked up. The knowledge of the EPIRB's efficacy raises my spirits somewhat, but in the back of my mind I have nagging doubts that anyone will hear mine. What about the Robertsons? In 1972 their nineteen-ton, forty-three-foot schooner was rammed and sunk by a whale. The family of five, plus one crew member, spent the next thirty-eight days adrift. Their inflatable raft lasted only seventeen days, but fortunately they also had a solid dinghy.

Worse yet, what about the Baileys? Like the Robertsons, their heavy cruiser was sunk by a whale and they were set adrift in the same area of the Pacific in two boats, both inflatable. The Baileys were rescued after 119 days, *nearly four months!* They are the only people to have survived longer than forty days in an inflatable raft; it is encouraging, though, to remember that both rafts lasted the entire ordeal.

What if my EPIRB is not heard? What if ships are scarce in the oceanic highways? Even if conditions are steady, it may take ninety days to reach the Caribbean, well over a hundred days if I'm swept north of eighteen degrees latitude. From Hierro I wrote to my parents that I might arrive in Antigua as late as March 10, thirty-four days from now. No one will search for me before then, if they ever search at all. Just one other man in history has survived alone and adrift for over a month. Poon Lim lived in a solid raft for an astounding 130 days after his ship was torpedoed during World War II. One hundred and thirty days! Don't think about it. Twenty days . . . Someone will see me within twenty days. A chart of normal air traffic routes would be most useful to determine when to use the EPIRB. I'll leave it on for thirty hours. That'll allow any daily flight twenty-four hours to hear, and six hours for search aircraft to reach me.

What kept the Baileys, the Robertsons, and Poon Lim alive? Experience, preparation, equipment, and luck. I'm doing well on the first three counts. Although most of the others started with more food and water than I have, I am well equipped with fishing gear. Although all of the others were adrift in areas of frequent rainfall, I have solar stills. I also have the benefit of their experience, especially the Robertsons', for I carry the survival book that Dougal Robertson wrote. Perhaps my biggest worry is that I have no replacement or backup for my single rubber raft. It will take extreme luck to keep it together for more than a month. I remember a film I saw when I was young, *You Make Your Luck.* I've got to do the best I can, the very best. I cannot shirk or procrastinate. I cannot withdraw. That torn blue desert outside will not accommodate me. I have often hidden things from myself. I have sometimes fooled other people.

But Nature is not such a dolt. I may be lucky enough to be forgiven some mistakes, the ones that don't matter, but I can't count on luck. Yet even if I show the skill and determination of the Baileys or Robertsons, I may die. How many others with greater skill and more determination have not returned to tell their tale?

Any loss of equipment can hammer the last nail into my coffin. Without water I can last a maximum of ten days. Without the air pump my raft will deflate and I'll last only hours. Should I lose even bits of paper or plastic, I might be unable to make a repair or device that could spell the difference between life and death. I double-tie my emergency equipment duffel to the life-lines. Into it I put every item of primary importance, especially the air pump. The raft requires periodic topping up. It slowly leaks air, primarily as the sun heats the black tubes and excess pressure is released through the valves. There is a small foot pump, similar to those used to blow up air matresses, with a long hose that plugs into the valves. It seems an odd pump for a raft, because one cannot stand up to pump it and the rippling floor is not solid enough to press the pump against it by hand. Instead, I grasp it with my hands and squeeze, feeling lucky that my hands are relatively large and strong.

The original raft equipment bag is tied to tabs on the floor. To make my home more secure and keep the interior warm, I cut holes in the tent flap, poke through bits of line, and tie the flap shut. I can do no more except conserve energy, hope the EPIRB is heard, and take stock of my surroundings.

The change from my dry, well-equipped little ship, *Napoleon Solo,* is staggering, unbelievable. Perhaps it is a nightmare from which I will awaken. But the water beating up under my back, the wind howling above me, the waves crashing around me, the cold, soaking caress of my bed, smack of reality with a clarity I've not known before.

Another eternity of night passes and the thirtieth hour arrives. I turn off the EPIRB. I did not think it would work. My next opportunity will be when I reach New York–South Africa shipping lanes. Air traffic routes often follow shipping lanes. But this lane will give me a poor chance at best, since New York to South Africa is a very long way to fly direct. By the time I am within range of the lanes, however, poor chances may look promising. Even if the EPIRB isn't picked up by a jet, I may be spotted by ships in the lanes. I figure it's a one-in-a-million shot to reach the lanes and another one-in-a-million to get spotted once I get there.

Often I think I hear a low hum that sounds like a plane. I get up and look about. Nothing. Wind fills my ears. Nothing.

FEBRUARY 6
DAY 2

Back inside, the noise is sometimes distinct; I feel sure it is not my imagination. I turn on the EPIRB again for several hours, then operate it periodically until thirty-six hours of use have passed. Save the rest. It must not be a plane. It must be the wind blowing on the raft's tubes. This constant phantom voice is a reminder of how little I can see from my little cave. I wonder how many ships and planes will pass me unawares?

I rip open a tin of peanuts and eat them slowly, savoring each nut. It is February 6, my birthday. This is not quite the meal I had planned. I have lived a nice, round thirty years. What have I to show for it? I write my own epitaph.

STEVEN CALLAHAN
FEBRUARY 6, 1952   FEBRUARY 6, 1982
Dreamed
Drew Pictures
Built Boats
Died

All that I have accomplished in life seems very trite and offers as little comfort as the bare horizon outside.

For three days the gale howls. Waves glitter in the sun and the wind blows white beards of froth down their blue chests.

During the day the sun brings a small spot of warmth to my frigid world. At night the wind and sea rear up more viciously. Even in these subtropical conditions, the water temperature falls below sixty-five degrees, so I risk dying from hypothermia before the sun rises. Naked and sore, wrapped in clammy foil and a sodden sleeping bag, I shiver and can sleep only in snatches, as my whole world rumbles and shakes. Waves breaking nearby and on the raft actually sound like cannon shot.

Continually drenched with salt water, my skin has broken out with hundreds of boils. They multiply quickly under my wet T-shirt and sleeping bag. Gouges and abrasions cover my lower spine, butt, and knees. They are foul, but I suppose they are clean. I'm often awakened with the searing pain of salt burning their putrid tenderness. The raft is too small for me to stretch out in, so I must rest curled up on my side. At least this helps to keep the cuts dry.

I discover two small holes in the floor, which explains the constant dribble of water into the raft. I probably sat on my knife when I abandoned ship. That would also explain some of the lacerations in my lower back. The patching kit contains glue and pieces of raft material. The instructions tell me to make sure the raft is dry before applying patches to it. Good joke! I plug the holes with small pieces of plastic and lumps of glue from the patching kit, and the floor is momentarily dry. But beads of water find their way around the plugs; the glue doesn't adhere to damp rubber. After three attempts and two hours of work, using tape, Band-Aids, and a lighter, I finally get a patch to stick, more or less. With the continuous thrashing and incessant wetness, I can't be assured it will hold but the relative dryness lifts my spirits. Now that I can slowly dry out, life within these rubber walls improves considerably. I have risen, if briefly, from my death bed.

I have seen many cruisers that travel with a minimum amount of emergency gear. I am prepared better than most. The raft's equipment bag is packed with:

- Six pints of water in tins with a couple of plastic lids. I can use them as storage containers later.
- Two short plywood paddles. I'm not about to stroke to the Caribbean, but I may be able to use them to drive off sharks.
- Two hand-launched parachute flares, three hand-held red flares, and two hand-held orange smoke flares.
- Two sponges.
- A folding radar reflector made to be mounted on a pole. There is no pole. And even *Solo,* with two reflectors fifteen feet off the deck, was not always picked up on radar, so I doubt the utility of this object.
- Two solar distillation units: solar stills.
- Two can openers, a broken medicine cup, and seasickness pills.
- A first aid kit, the contents of which are the only dry thing in the bag.
- A rubber collapsible basin.
- A 100-foot, ⅛-inch polypropylene heaving line.
- Survival charts, protractor, pencil, and eraser.
- A flashlight and two signal mirrors.
- Raft patching kit: glue, rubber patches, and conical, screw-like plugs.
- So-called fishing kit: fifty feet of twine and one medium hook.

Also tied to the raft is a dull-tipped knife. The theory is that the raft won't be accidentally punctured. However, the blade won't cut much of anything. Cleaning a fish with it would be tantamount to operating with a baseball bat.

I am very glad to have my own emergency duffel. In it I have:
- A Tupperware box with pencils, dime-store pads of paper, plastic mirrors, protractor, sheath knife, pocket knife, stainless-steel utensil kit, sail twine, hooks, codline, 3/16-inch line, two chemical light sticks, and the book *Sea Survival,* by Dougal Robertson. The contents of the box are the only other dry things in the raft.

- Space blanket, now unpacked—the foil in which I wrap myself. The shiny, thin foil traps body heat and reflects it back onto the person it covers.
- Plastic bags.
- Another solar still.
- Some plugs made of pine for patching holes.
- Another 100-foot heaving line.
- Assorted stainless-steel shackles.
- Assorted line: approximately 100 feet of ⅛ inch, 100 feet of ¼ inch, plus the 70 feet of ⅜ inch tied to the man-overboard pole, which trails astern.
- The EPIRB, now unpacked.
- A Very pistol with twelve red parachute flares, three red meteor flares, two hand-held orange smoke flares, three hand-held red flares, one hand-held white flare.
- Two pints of water in a plastic jug.
- Two pieces of ⅛-inch plywood to use as cutting boards.
- Two pintles and two gudgeons: fittings for a boat's rudder.
- A short spear gun.
- A bag with food: ten ounces of peanuts, sixteen ounces of baked beans, ten ounces of corned beef, and ten ounces of soaked raisins.
- A small strobe light.

In addition I have saved the small piece of closed-cell foam cushion, one and a half one-pound cabbages, a piece of mains'l, the man-overboard pole and horseshoe, my sleeping bag, and a leather knife.

I had bought Dougal Robertson's survival book on sale years ago. It's worth a king's ransom to me now. The spear gun I had bought in the Canaries. It didn't fit well anywhere in *Solo*. After smacking my head against it several times, I had lighted upon the idea of trying to fit it into my emergency duffel. With the arrow removed and a small amount of tugging and shoving, it finally slid inside. That it did will prove to be incredibly good fortune.

I begin to keep notes on my state of health, the raft's condition, and the quantity of food and water. I also keep a navigational record and begin to write a log. "I have lost all but my past, my friends, and of course the shirt off my back. Ho, ho. Will I make it? I don't know." I write as steadily as I can on dime-store three-by-five-inch pads. Even this simple task takes great effort, as the raft continually lurches about. I take the notes out only when I'm sure that the raft will not be capsized or flooded. When I am done, I double-bag them in plastic, each bag carefully tied, combine them with my survival manual in another plastic bag, and put them in my equipment duffel.

Presuming that the raft stays intact, and I acquire no additional food or water, I can last at best until February 22, fourteen more days. I may just reach the shipping lanes, where I will have a remote chance of being spotted. Dehydration will take its toll by that time. My tongue will swell until it fills my mouth and then will blacken. My eyes will be sucked deeply into my head. Death will knock at the door to my delirious mind.

An eternity exists between the click of each second. I remind myself that time does not stand still. The seconds will stack up like poker chips. Seconds into minutes, minutes into hours, hours into days. Time *will* pass. In months I will look back on this hell from a comfortable seat in the future . . . perhaps, if I am lucky.

Desperation shakes me. I want to cry but I scold myself. Hold it back. Choke it down. You cannot afford the luxury of water wept away. I bite my lips, close my eyes, and weep within. Survival, concentrate on survival. Clear sea stretches for two miles under me. No life is visible in the depths from which I might score a meal. It is too rough to use the solar stills in the water. For now I can hope only to be found.

The man-overboard pole cuts a wake astern. Its bright flag rises to the top of each wave as the raft is lost in the trough. That should improve my visibility to passing ships. If *Solo* is still floating I have twice the chance of someone stumbling over my debris. It is a small thing, but now small things are all I have. "Cheap thrills are better than no thrills at all," echoes in my head. Somehow my jokes are not funny. I no longer smile, but I continue to make light of whatever I can in order to relieve the tension.

There is little to do now except keep watch and daydream. My life keeps passing before my eyes in intricate detail, like a grade B movie rerun too often. I try to shift my thoughts to the things that I want to do if I am saved. I will spend more time with my parents and friends, let them know that I love them. Daydreams of future plans, of being home, of boat and life raft designs, and of big happy meals ease my desperation. Stop it! You are not there. You are here, in purgatory. Do not give yourself false hope. Think about survival!

But the desire to dream lingers. It is my one relief. I slowly come to terms with the disappointments of my past and I begin to see that I have had some valuable experience and training, possibly even enough to survive this. If I can pull through, I will be able to lead a better life. And even if I don't see my thirty-first year, maybe I can make this time useful. My writings may be found aboard the raft, even if I am dead. They might be instructive to others, especially those who sail and might find themselves in a similar situation. It's the last service I can render. Dreams, ideas, and plans not only are an escape, they give me purpose, a reason to hang on.

The morning of February 8 brings a slight calming of the gale. Waves continue rolling down upon us, some still fifteen feet or more in height. But they have FEBRUARY 8 lost their curling heads and do not smash the DAY 4 raft as often. I look out across the liquid desert. There is no oasis, no water to drink or shading palms. Like a desert, there *is* life here, but it has evolved over millenniums to survive without fresh water.

A small piece of sargasso weed floats by to the north. Sargasso, tumbleweed of the oceans, grows without roots and floats freely across the surface. The great Sargasso Sea lies to the northwest, where legend has it that hundreds of aging hulks are trapped in the weeds' masses. But there is little of it here. Pity; it could serve to judge my speed.

The waters of the world are in constant flux. Weather exists in the oceans just as it exists in the atmosphere. Undersea storms rip through the passes and canyons between underwater mountain ranges. Windflow across the earth's surface affects and mirrors the waterflow of great ocean currents. In some areas the ocean lies barely moving, virtually parked. In others it flows like traffic on a highway. These great water roads include the Gulf Stream, and the Agulhas, Humboldt, South Equatorial, Indian Monsoon, and Labrador currents. Some travel at more than fifty miles a day. I am traveling a slower path, the North Equatorial, at six to twelve miles a day. It runs steadily with the wind toward the Caribbean.

As if stepping on the accelerator, the wind thrusts me into the passing lane. I can sail faster than the water traffic. My chart of the Indian Ocean is of little use to me, so I rip it up. After soaking the crumpled balls to prevent them from being blown by the wind, I watch them float away. Just at the surface, they take more than two minutes to reach the man-overboard pole. It is seventy feet astern, or one-ninetieth of a nautical mile. This crude speedometer shows that I'm moving only eight miles each day over the water. Including current, at seventeen miles a day average, it will take me another twenty-two days to reach the lanes. It is too long, way too long. It is time to move.

I pull up the sea anchor, which pulses through the water like a jellyfish and tows the ocean behind. I make sure it's ready to reset at a moment's notice should waves threaten to capsize us. Now the raft rides better, yielding more easily to punches as it slowly glides ahead. My speed is now twenty-five to thirty miles per day. It is still a long way to the shipping lanes, but with the increase in speed, I feel a glimmer of optimism. At least now *theoretically* I can make it.

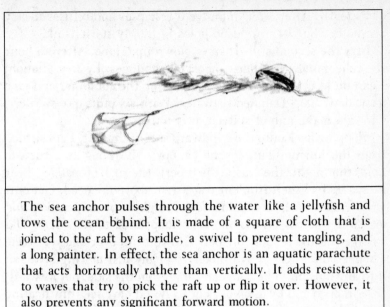

The sea anchor pulses through the water like a jellyfish and tows the ocean behind. It is made of a square of cloth that is joined to the raft by a bridle, a swivel to prevent tangling, and a long painter. In effect, the sea anchor is an aquatic parachute that acts horizontally rather than vertically. It adds resistance to waves that try to pick the raft up or flip it over. However, it also prevents any significant forward motion.

I mark my one-liter clear plastic water jug with shallow knife cuts and ration myself to one-half pint of water per day. To take only a mouthful every six hours or so is difficult discipline. I have decided not to drink seawater. Dougal Robertson and most survival experts advise that it is too dangerous. It may provide immediate relief, but the high level of sodium must be urinated away, drawing even more fluid from the body's tissues, soon leaving a withered corpse.

I try to use the first solar still. It is an inflatable balloon that is supposed to evaporate seawater. In sunny, tropical, calm conditions, it should produce two pints of fresh water from seawater each day. That's one to two days' worth of minimal survival rations. When I blow this balloon up and put it in the water as instructed, it travels at about the same speed as the raft. Sometimes we thump into one another. Sometimes it surfs ahead on a passing wave until it comes to a staggering halt at the end of its leash. After a few minutes it collapses and refuses to stay reinflated, but I can find no holes in it. My spirits sink.

I try the second still. It stays blown up. Hope. After an hour the collection bag contains almost eight ounces of water. Elation! I can build up my water stock! I pick up the container and take a swallow. Salt! Damned seawater! With six pints of water left, I have a maximum of sixteen days to live.

Flopping back onto the windward side of the raft, I am shaded from the burning sun by the canopy. My thoughts return to *Solo,* that night, the crash, the report, the rush of water. I hear it, see it, feel the turbulent water rise above my head. Get out, she's going down . . . going *down!* A ghost of desperation and loss wafts across my vision. What happened to you, *Solo?* Did I make you too tender, my pet? Did you run over a log or strike a truck container? It is unlikely that my fast-moving boat ran into any flotsam. The collision came from the side, not forward. *Solo* stopped and I was on deck quickly. I'd have seen any floating debris big enough to cause such devastation. Something big, moving fast, must have run into us. No ships were visible from the deck. It was something from the sea itself.

A big one. Maybe a whale. A few years ago I ran a thirty-five-foot trimaran into a forty-foot sperm whale in the Gulf Stream. For the owner aboard it was the second such encounter in as many trips to Bermuda in the same year. We were fortunate. One hull smacked down on top of the skin-covered island, but neither the whale nor the boat was permanently damaged. The Robertsons and the Baileys, though, were both sunk by whales. Feeding near the surface at night when the bigger plankton come up, a cetacean would not have noticed *Solo's* hull cutting silently through the noisy breaking of the sea. A moderate-size thirty-five tonner striking *Solo's* side at ten knots would have caused substantial damage, although the collision would not even have disturbed the whale's feeding routine.

I have seen so many of them—playful porpoise, curious pilots, great fins, and strong sperm. They emerge from the depths without warning. Suddenly there's a huge beast there. And at that moment a profound emotion—not fear—rises from the depths of my soul. It is like seeing a friend whom I thought I'd never see again, who miraculously appears and who may just as suddenly disappear forever. Whenever these massive spirits appear from the depths, I feel a wonderful electricity in the air, an aura of immense intelligence and sensitivity. In this momentary meeting, I feel the greatness of this friend's life and soul.

I do not like the fact that whales are hunted, but then again, I often think that the beautiful "balance of nature" is really just everything running around eating each other. And in some ways I envy the Azorians and Eskimos who hunt whales with hand-thrown harpoons from small boats. They must get dangerously close to their prey; and when the odds are even for the hunter and the hunted, they must become bound in a unique brotherhood of understanding.

I look down at the slab of whale tooth that hangs from a string around my neck. What of this token? I am a small part Cherokee Indian. My mind turns to the customs of my forebears, the use of trinkets that linked them to their counterparts in nature—eagle feathers, bear claws. What is more fitting for me to wear than a reminder of the great spirits of the sea? Is it coincidence that I should feel so close to whales, wear the jewelry of their death and be tried by them? Or has it a deeper . . . No. I don't believe in that. Out of the infinite number of events that happen every second, many must be surrounded by odd circumstance. Yet life must be nourished with meaning just as with food, and stories give events meaning. I reach for the most unique and surprising: strange coincidence, long shot, miracle. I need a tale of miracles. Can I reap a legend from this chapter of my life? Is the whale my totem, my animal counterpart? Is this a test of that totem, a test of the whale within me?

Six pints of water are left. Is it enough for another sixteen days? Perhaps I can catch some rain. Just hang on for twenty days. As long as the raft does not get damaged, I have a chance.

Suddenly a fin slashes through the surface in front of the

raft. I leap to the opening, fumbling with one of the paddles to beat it off. I see the svelte, cool blue form cruising under me. It doesn't struggle to pace us. As the next wave passes, clouding my view, the form rockets ahead and is lost to sight. He is small, a four-foot oceanic bullet. Out of the corner of my eye I see the slice of another fin, racing down the face of the next wave. It cuts diagonally toward me and shoots by just in front. It is not a shark. It is a fish. A fish! It is one beautiful, food-filled, sweet blue fish!

Quickly rummaging through my emergency bag, I claw out the spear gun and arrow. Wait . . . what if it is a strong fish? I hurriedly tie a piece of line through the gun handle and onto the raft. My stomach growls. Four days on a pound of food. I'm trembling with excitement.

I must watch the waves. With my weight on the low side, a breaker might easily capsize us. At times I must leap back to windward and hang on until the foaming eruption subsides. Meanwhile I observe the dorados. They are three to four feet long and must weigh twenty to thirty pounds. Their power will make them difficult to catch. A sailor in the Canaries once told me of a dorado that knocked a boat's cockpit to pieces, including a bolted-down steering-wheel pedestal. A continuous dorsal fin stretches from the squared-off head down the aquamarine back to a bright, yellow-finned tail. It is their tails that are visible from far away, piercing the surface as they bodysurf down waves. These fish are widely renowned for agility, strength, beauty— and good eating.

I've never caught one or even seen one in the ocean before. The sea is obviously not a threat to *them*. It is their home, their playground. A few cruise by about six feet away, just out of range. But in their curiosity they swing close every now and then. Surface refraction makes it difficult to aim, and the lurching raft is a poor platform from which to shoot. My few attempts miss widely. Hunger continues to gnaw as the sun sets.

Another two days bring more sun, wind, sea, and dorados. Leaping out of the sea in ten-foot arcs and landing on their sides, they look like agile, breeching whales. I'd drool if only my mouth could summon more than sticky saliva. "Come my beauties, come just a bit closer," I coo to them. But when they approach, my spear misses the mark.

My mind creates fantasies of food and drink and turns continually back to *Solo,* to the pounds of fruits, nuts, and vegetables and the gallons of water within her. I see myself opening lockers and pulling out food. I plan how I might have saved her, shifted stores, dumped ballast, raised her in midocean to sail again. What if we hadn't become separated? What if we hadn't left the Canaries? What if . . . Stop it! She's gone. Concentrate on *now,* on survival.

Once again I try one of the solar stills. As it sails forward, its water collection bag drags behind on the surface. This prevents the fresh water from draining into it. So I must frequently empty the balloon of a small amount of water. The day's total is one-half pint. Seas continue to batter the still until the tabs that hold its tether are ripped off. I often dump out the water to find it is salty. My body's craving for water is building. I would give anything for a drink, but can only afford an occasional mouthful. I open my first can of fresh water. Five pints left, maybe fifteen days to live if I can catch fresh fish to supplement my fluid intake. Otherwise I may have as little as ten days left.

At least things are drying out and at night I can sleep. I escape through dreams. Each hour I awake to my prison, my hair pulled out by the chafing rubber, my joints aching for the chance to stretch out.

On February 10, my sixth day in the raft, the wind blows hard as the Atlantic continues "the shuffle," a term sailors use for the commonly confused wave **FEBRUARY 10** patterns of the Atlantic. Ridges of waves ap- **DAY 6** proach from the northeast, east, and southeast. They break on three sides of the raft, tumbling it about in a nonstop rock-and-roll dance. At least we are headed more westerly, more directly toward the West Indies.

But with each good thing comes the bad. The repair to the

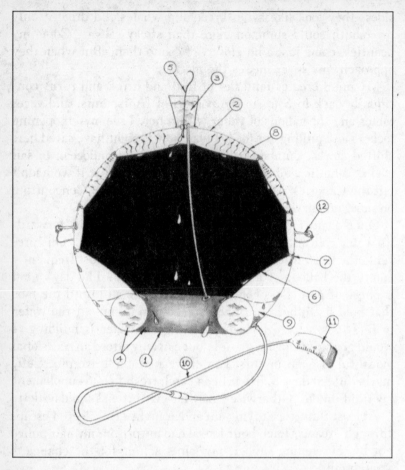

floor has come up, and after hesitating to use some of the last patching equipment, I manage to seal it. I feel weak. The still produces only salt-ridden water, and I argue with myself not to drink more than one-half pint of my reserve each day. The dorados are beautiful but tease me by staying just out of range with quick evasive maneuvers. One passes close by and I fire. The spear jerks my arm straight. It's hit! The raft twists around. Then the fish is gone. The silver arrow lies limp, dangling from the end of its rope, too weak to drive through these fish. Hunger

THE SOLAR STILL. The stills that I use are military surplus models. They are no longer manufactured, but other stills work on similar principles. My stills are rated to produce a maximum of thirty-two ounces of fresh water per day, a two-day survival ration. I get thirty ounces on the best days and often as little as sixteen.

A cloth bottom (1) allows excess seawater to seep through. When wet, it is airtight and allows the plastic balloon (2) to be inflated. Seawater is poured into the reservoir (3) on the top. The first half gallon drains down a tube into the salt water ballast ring (4). Additional seawater drips from the reservoir through a tiny valve. A jiggle string (5) keeps the valve free and helps regulate flow. From the valve, the seawater drops onto a black cloth wick (6). The wick is suspended from the sides of the balloon by attachment loops (7), which keep the wick away from the balloon; otherwise salt water from the wick will drain onto the balloon's inner surface and pollute the distillate. The black wick becomes saturated with seawater. Some of the seawater evaporates. The vapor, shown by squiggly arrows, collects as small drops of fresh water (8) on the inside of the balloon. The drops trickle down to the fresh water, or distillate, reservoir (9). From here the water drains down a tube (10) into the distillate collection bag (11). The tube is equipped with a fitting that allows removal of the bag for emptying. The bag is weighted with a piece of lead for proper drainage. A skirt and lanyard (12) pass around the middle of the still. Although the still is designed to be used in the water, I must use mine aboard the raft.

is eating my fat, then it will eat my muscles, then my mind.

I bend over the tubes and look down deep into the sea. There are no fish, no weeds, only empty blue. Have I missed my only chance to catch food? Have they gone? Suddenly a shape appears forty yards to the side, gliding with incredible speed right for the raft. A ten-foot beige body with an unmistakable broad hammerhead tells me all I need to know. Man-eater. No dorsal fin rips through the water. Its long, sleek torso needs hardly move to thrust itself ahead. My heart pounds. I hold my spear tightly. If I shoot I will lose the arrow. I gaze at the shark sliding under me just below the surface. Making a smooth, tight corner, it circles back, faster now. As if accelerated by centrifugal force, it closes in on the raft. My mouth is dry, my arms shake; cold sweat streams from my skin. A complete circle executed, the beast thrusts into the wind and melts into the blue as quickly as it came. The vision will last forever. How often will they come? I will never dare to swim from the raft.

I wonder about God. Do I believe in Him? Somehow I cannot accept a vision of a super humanoid, but I believe in the miraculous and spiritual way of things—existence, nature, the universe. I do not know the true workings of that way. I can only guess and hope that it includes me.

Nothing seems to hold a future. The horseshoe preserver chafes on the raft tubes. I am already pumping air into them four times a day to keep them properly inflated. Additional wear can mean disaster. I decide to use the float to make "bottles" and to write messages for my bottles. I cut the float in half, spewing snowy styrofoam nubs all around the raft, wrap my desperate letters in plastic bags, and tape them to the styrofoam blocks. "Situation poor, prognosis worse, approximate position . . . direction and speed of drift . . . please notify and give my love to . . ." I cast them out upon the waters and watch them tumble southward. Perhaps someone will see them. If *Solo* lives, there are four remnants of me that can be found.

It is my eleventh day in the raft. Each day passes as an endless age of despair. I spend hours evaluating my chances, my strength, and my distance to the lanes. The raft's condition seems generally good, although the tent leaks through the observation port when nearby waves break. One night we shot down the front of a big roller, for several seconds sliding upon its tumbling foam as if we had fallen over a waterfall. Then last night we nearly capsized again. Everything is soaked. Today, though, a flat, hot sea surrounds me. The sun beats

FEBRUARY 15
DAY 11

down on the wide expanse of this liquid frying pan and things begin to dry out once more. The sun and sedate sea are welcome.

My scabs are torn off or wiped away when my skin is wet. With the sun they will heal, eventually. Most of the salt water boils have vanished. There is a great emptiness in my stomach, a cramped, incessant yearning. It visits me each night in my dreams. Fantasies of hot-fudge sundaes with numerous varieties of ice cream dance through my head. Last night I nearly got to taste hot buttered whole-wheat biscuits, but they were snatched away from me when I woke up. And how many hours have I spent back on *Solo*, collecting the dried fruit, the fruit juices, the nuts? Hunger is a witch from whom there is no escape. Her spells conjure these visions of food and deepen the pain. I look at my stock. The can of beans is blown. I dare not eat them for fear of botulism. Then again, maybe they're all right. Quickly now, pitch them! Do it, I tell you! The can lands with a sickening kerplunk. I'm left with two cabbage stems and wet, fermented raisins in a plastic bag. The stems are slimy and bitter. I eat them anyway.

A smaller variety of fish has appeared. About twelve inches long, they have tiny, tight round mouths and little flippers like hands waving on the top and bottom of their bodies. Their big round eyes roll as they dart under the raft and peck at the bottom with their strong jaws. Are they trying to eat it? They must be the tough-skinned triggerfish. Reef triggers eat corals and are considered poisonous, but survivors have often eaten triggers from the open ocean with no ill effects. Anything would be good to eat, anything to stop the gnawing in my gut. I may soon go mad, eat paper, drink the sea.

Often when I have gone offshore, I have found myself to be somewhat schizophrenic, though not dysfunctional. I see myself divide into three basic parts; physical, emotional, and rational. It's common for solo sailors to talk to themselves, to ask for a second opinion about how to deal with a problem. You try to think as another person, to get a new outlook and to talk yourself into positive action. When I am in danger or injured, my emotional self feels fear and my physical self feels pain. I instinctively rely on my rational self to take command over the fear and pain. This tendency is increasing as my voyage lengthens. The lines that stretch between my commanding rational self and my frightened emotional and vulnerable physical selves is getting tighter and tighter. My rational commander relies on hope, dreams, and cynical jokes to relieve the tension in the rest of me.

In my log I write: "The dorados remain, beautiful, alluring. I ask one to marry me. But her parents will not hear of it. I am not colorful enough. Imagine, bigotry even here! However, they also point out that I do not have a very bright future. It is a reasonable objection."

Watching the fish makes my stomach ache more. I continue to fail at fishing. I manage to spear a triggerfish but it jerks free. I make a lure by tying together hooks, white nylon webbing, and aluminum foil, then stuffing it with a precious morsel of corned beef. A dorado strikes hard and bites effortlessly through the heavy codline. This fish is now easy to recognize, with the long line trailing from his mouth. I have no wire leader to catch these fish by hook and line so I must rely on the spear.

Finally my aim is true. The spear strikes home. A dorado erupts with resistance and thrashes wildly. I fumble for the spear, try to keep the tip away from the raft, and haul the fish aboard. Just as I get it to the edge, a final convulsion turns fury to escape. Perhaps I can live twenty more days without food.

If hunger is the witch, thirst is her curse. It is nagging, screaming thirst that causes me to watch each minute pass, to wait for the next sip. I've had only one cup of water for each of the first nine days. Daytime temperatures are in the eighties or nineties. Hours pass between single swallows of water. To keep cool and reduce sweating, I pour seawater over myself. Dry wind bites my lips. A light rain fell one evening, but its mist quickly dried. The winds here have come from America in a long and roundabout route. They first travel north and east until they reach Europe. Then they sweep south, depositing rain along the way. By the time they have reached this latitude, they are headed back west and have had most of the moisture wrung out of them. Some of the air is as dry as the Sahara over which it has recently passed. Rainfall will be rare until the winds cross enough sea to be fed by its evaporation, which will be well to the west of where I am now.

The second solar still deflates after being torn by the waves. It had never worked properly. What is wrong with them? I begin thinking of an onboard still—the Tupperware box, with cans inside. If I can get water to evaporate from the cans, water vapor might collect on a tentlike cover and drip down into the box. To draw more heat and increase evaporative surface area in the cans, I decide to fill them with crumpled black cloth from one of the solar stills. If I take a still apart, I may be able to find out what the problem is. I'll lose a still, but they are no good as they are. So I cut one up. I find that salt water contamination is coming from the black cloth's hitting the plastic balloon's sides when the still is not fully inflated. Excessive shaking in rough seas may also be spraying salt water from the black cloth wick into the distilled fresh water. So it is not a single problem; it requires multiple solutions. I must find and plug any holes in the balloons and stabilize the stills.

My onboard still is a dismal failure. The evaporation rate is much too slow and the system too ventilated to allow condensation on the box lid. At least I get the last still to work by tying it close to the raft so that it isn't flung about by waves; however, it chafes there. Why not try it aboard the raft? I pull it up onto the edge of the top tube and tie it in place. The balloon sags a little, but it stays put and the wick isn't touching the plastic. Drainage of the distilled water is also improved, because the distillate collection bag hangs down rather than trailing out horizontally. I watch as pure, clear, unsalted drops begin to

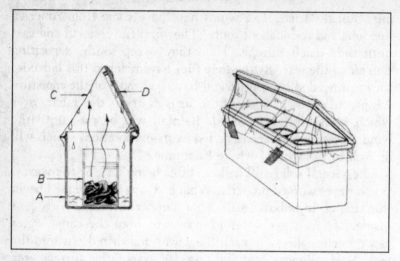

collect and drain into the bag. I have her working! And I have three pints of reserve . . . possibly I can make it! After eleven days, I have renewed hope. As long as the raft holds together and the still functions, I can last another twenty days. The raft . . . Please, no sharks. I am not only worried about their rows of jagged teeth. Their skins are like coarse sandpaper; they can rip my raft apart just by rubbing against it.

I lie back in the healing heat of the sun. There is an abundance of time, a bumper crop of it, in which to think. Dorados and triggerfish nudge the raft's bottom. Baby gooseneck barnacles have begun to flourish on it. The triggers feed on them. I don't know why the dorados are bumping. They begin in the evenings, at about dusk, firmly nudging wherever I or my equipment push into the floor. It is as if they were dogs pushing their begging heads under a human hand for a piece of meat, a scratch behind the ear, or a playmate. I call them my little doggies or doggie heads. The triggers I call butlers. They have that starched-collar look.

The sea lies flat. Clouds sit motionless in the sky as if glued there. The sun beats down, roasting my arid body. The working

I attempt to make an onboard solar still. Perspective view, *right*. Section, *left:* (A) The Tuppeware box. (B) I place three empty water cans in the box. In each I crumple black cloth from the solar still that I cut up and wet it with seawater. The cloth should soak up more heat and give more surface area for evaporation than seawater simply floating in the cans. Theoretically, fresh water vapor should rise and collect on the plastic tent that I've taped over the front and ends (C) as well as the box lid (D), and then drip down the sides and collect in the box bottom around the outside of the cans. The experiment is a depressing failure. I don't have enough tape to seal the tent to the box thoroughly, and the tape does not stick well to the slippery box. Therefore, excessive ventilation on the inside of the tent prevents moisture from collecting.

still may provide just enough water to carry me the three hundred miles to the shipping lanes. The wind has turned. The lanes somehow always seem to be three hundred miles away. As I succumb to drowsiness, fantasies of being picked up by a ship and lying in the cool green grass by the pond at my parents' house race through my head.

The shaking of the raft jerks me from my stupor. I look down. A flat, gray, round-headed beast scrapes its hide across the bottom as it lazily swings around for another bite. It's incredible that the dorados and triggers have not fled the shark at all! Instead, they collect closely around it. I think they have invited him for tea. "Come over to our place and have a taste of this big black crumpet." He slowly swims around to the stern and slides under. Rolling over, belly up, he bites one of the ballast pockets, quaking the raft with his convulsive ten-foot torso. Bless the pockets. He might tear a hole in the floor, but that shouldn't damage the tubes, at least not yet. Should I take a shot and risk losing the spear? He cruises out in front of me just below the surface. I thrust, and the steel strikes his back. It is like hitting stone. With one quick stroke he slithers away, not in any particular hurry. I watch for a long time before collapsing, craving water more than ever.

I thought that the fish would scatter and give me notice of a shark's approach, but now I know that I cannot trust them to warn me of danger. I worry about the gas bottle and line that inflated the raft and that lie under the bottom tube. If that line is bitten through, will the whole raft deflate? Will the bottle lure the sharks to bite into the tube from which it hangs? Worry, worry, worry. It is apprehension that beds with me each night and apprehension that awakens me each day. As darkness comes and I drift off to sleep, I long to be in a place with no anxieties. How repetitious and simple my desires have become.

The raft is lifted and thrown to the side as if kicked by a giant's boot. A shark's raking skin scrapes a squeak from it as I leap from slumber. "Keep off the bottom!" I yell at myself as I pull the cushion and sleeping bag close to the opening. I perch as lightly as possible upon it. Peering into the night, I grasp the spear gun. He's on the other side. I must wait until he comes to the opening. A fin breaks the water in a quick swirl of phosphorescent fire and darts behind the raft, circling in to strike again. A flicker of light in the black sea shows me he is below, and I jab with a splash. Nothing. Damn! The splash may entice him to attack more viciously. Again the fin cuts the surface. The shark smashes into the raft with a rasping blow. I strike at the flicker. Hit! The water erupts, the dark fin shoots out and around and then is gone. Where is he? My heart's pounding breaks the silence. It beats across the still black waters to the stars. I wait.

Gulping a half pint of water, I rearrange my bed so that at the first bump I can be ready at the entrance. Hours pass before I drift again into uneasy sleep.

For two days the going is slow under the baking sky. I go fourteen or fifteen miles each twenty-four hours. Hunger wrenches my insides. My mouth burns. But the still produces twenty ounces of water a day. I begin to rebuild my stock while drinking

My heart's pounding beats across the still black
waters to the stars.

one pint for each arc of the sun. The calm is also good for
visibility. Should a ship pass, the glowing orange canopy will be
more easily spotted. However, sharks also visit more frequently
in calm weather. The shipping lanes lie over two weeks to the
west at this pace. For hours I pore over the chart, estimating
minimum and maximum time and distance to rescue.

In my thirteen days adrift, I have eaten only three pounds of
food. My stomach is in knots, but starvation is more subtle than
simply increasing pain. My movements are slower, more fatiguing. The fat is gone. Now my muscles feed on themselves.
Visions of food snap at me like whips. I feel little else.

Several triggerfish swim up from astern as the breeze builds.
They come up broadside. Once again I aim and fire. The spear

strikes and drives through. I yank the impaled fish aboard. Its tight round mouth belches a clicking croak. Its eyes roll wildly. The stiff, rough body can only flap its fins in protest. Food! Lowering my head I chant, "Food, I have food." Shrinkage of the codline around the cutting board has warped a trough into it. I wedge the trigger under the line in the trough and try to strike it unconscious with my flare gun. It's like clubbing concrete. Powerful thrusts with my knife finally penetrate the trigger's armored skin. Its eyes flash, its fins frantically wave about, its throat cracks, and finally it is dead. My eyes fill with tears. I weep for my fish, for me, for the state of my desperation. Then I feed on its bitter meat.

DREAM KEEP

proves to resemble a rhinoceros more than a butler. A thick, horny bone protrudes from its back. I pound on the handle butt of my sharp sheath knife, finally driving the point through the skin, which is as tough as cowhide and has a very rough coating that looks like ground-up glass.

I bury my face in the raw, wet flesh to suck up the brownish-red blood. Intense, revolting bitterness fills my mouth, and I spit it out. Hesitantly, I take an eye into my mouth, crush it between my teeth, and retch. No wonder even sharks steer clear of this fish.

Because of its tough hide, the little ocean rhino must be cleaned from the outside in—skinned, filleted, and finally gutted. My teeth tear at one, bitter, stringy fillet, tough as the proverbial boot, and I hang the other up to dry. Organ meats, especially the liver, are the only palatable morsels to be found. I think of a movie character who is a cranky, miserable old fart at the beginning, but who is finally understood and loved in the end. I have penetrated the distasteful, tough façade of the triggerfish to discover a savory richness in its inner being.

Once when I was a small boy in Massachusetts, a hurricane tore across the land. I remember thick oak trees waving about in the wind like blades of grass. My brother had built a sturdy treehouse high atop the limbs of one tree. The storm blew it to pieces. The power of that storm was awesome, but I had heard of stronger forces, atomic forces, that eclipsed such storms. I put five dollars, a jackknife, fishing reel, and associated paraphernalia into a box and secreted it in my desk drawer. If disaster struck, I would be ready. If anyone survived, it would be me. Such are the immortal fantasies of youth.

The small amount of food is little comfort to my bones, which are beginning to protrude from my atrophied muscles. Worse is a deep emptiness in my soul. I'm an ill-adapted intruder in this domain, and I have murdered one of its citizens. Death may be thrust upon me more quickly, more unexpectedly, even more naturally than it came to this fish. My weak physical and frightened emotional selves fear this. My strong rational self acknowledges that it would be simple justice. As I swallow the sweet liver, I search for a savior across the deserted waves. I am quite alone.

The gray overcast sky reflects a calm, bleak sea. Yesterday's sun allowed the solar still to conjure up twenty ounces of fresh water. Its magic will be less potent today. Clouds ease the roasting afternoon sun but deny me maximum water production. Life is full of paradoxes. When the wind blows hard, I move well toward my destination, but I am wet, cold, scared, and in danger of capsizing. When it is calm, I dry out, heal, and fish more easily, but my projected journey lengthens and my encounters with sharks increase. There are no good conditions in a life raft, and no comfortable positions in which to rest. There are only the bad and the worse, the uncomfortable and the less so.

Quick, hard punches batter my back and legs. It is not a shark, but a dorado. I am not surprised. Their nudging has grown more confident, almost violent, like a boxer's jab. Time and again they hit where any weight indents the floor of the raft. Perhaps they are feeding on barnacles. The projection makes it easy for them to get at the little nubs of barnacle meat that have begun to grow under me.

I have missed my targets so many times that I am slow to take aim. Punch, punch—it's a damned nuisance. The dorados circle in from ahead and take a wide sweep around the raft as if in a bombing pattern. I cannot stand up to watch their final approach and simultaneously ready myself with the spear, so I kneel, awaiting my chance to strike. They shoot out in front, to the side—too wide, too deep.

Casually I point the gun in the general direction of a swimming body. "Take that!" Thump. The fish lies stunned in the water. I too am stunned. I hoist him aboard. Foam, water, and blood erupt about his flailing tail. His clublike head twists spasmodically. All my strength goes into keeping the spear tip from ripping into my inflated ship as his heavy, thrashing body whips it about. I leap upon him and pin his head down onto the eighth-inch-thick plywood square that serves as my cutting board. A big round eye stares into mine. I feel his pain. The book says press the eyes to paralyze the fish. My captive's fury increases. Hesitantly I plunge my knife into the socket—even more fury. He's thrusting loose. Watch the spear tip. There is no time for sympathy. I fumble with my knife, stick it into his side, work it about, find the spine and crack it apart. His body quivers; his gaze dulls with death. I fall back; behold my catch. His body is no longer blue as when in the sea. Instead, my treasure has turned to silver.

Pandemonium now surrounds the raft. I have noticed that these fish often travel in pairs. My captive's mate strikes with unmitigated fury. I try to ignore the painful beatings for three hours while I clean my catch.

I cut the flesh into one-inch-square by six-inch-long strips. These I poke holes through and thread on strings to dry. As evening approaches I throw the head and bones as far away as I can and wash out the blood-soaked sponges as quickly as possible. Sharks can detect a single part of blood per millions of parts water, like smelling out a particular steak dinner among all of the dinner plates in Boston.

At least thirty fish gather for their nightly escort. They beat at the raft like a lynch mob buzzing with hatred. Silent murmurings reach my ears. "You will pay for your murder, human."

I yell back, "Leave me alone, why can't you just leave me alone?" Time and again I load my spear, jerk the powerful elastic, and blindly fire into their midst below the raft. Many are stung by the point of my argument. My arms tire. The spot on my chest where I rest the butt of the gun while loading is sore. Still, one fish cannot be driven off. Mechanically I eat a slab of her mate as I watch her wheel around in the clear water to strike me again and again. The flesh is not as delicious as I had anticipated. She continues to beat at me into the night.

FEBRUARY 18
DAY 14

Morning brings a change in flavor. The meat is superb, akin to swordfish or tuna. Perhaps it must age slightly. It deserves better treatment than I can give it, a bit of garlic and lemon, preparation in a proper kitchen. To stop eating is difficult, but I must. A long time may elapse before I catch another fish.

I sit a thousand miles away from any companionship, money, or luxury, yet I have a feeling of wealth. Fifteen pounds of raw fish dangle from clotheslines that I've rigged in one half of the raft. I call it the butcher shop. The solar still is beginning to glisten with condensation, coins tossed to this beggar by the aristocratic sun. It is not much, but the implications of my meager cache are great. Slowly I am evolving a home out of this rubber, string, and steel. My focus is not on any immediate danger but on long-term survival. Hunger has been satisfied, my thirst is tolerable. I can live at least ten days, enough to cover the 220 miles left between me and the shipping lanes. I can rest from fishing. The holes in my knees and rear end may heal by the time I reach the lanes, so I can then keep a closer lookout. Who would believe that I, chronic complainer and impatient man of the ages, would ever look upon a lump of raw fish and a pint of water as wealth?

Acting like a fisheye mirror, the shiny plastic solar still reflects a bleak sky coming upon the stern. Slowly the clear plastic of the still hazes with condensation, begins to drop its nectar, drip . . . drip . . . drip. I reflect on my future. "When I get home I will . . . I will . . . I will . . ."

I have always been a dreamer. When I was four, my parents gave me a toy castle with bright red and blue uniformed soldiers. The threads of their lives lay in a bundle of plywood and lead from which I could spin many tales. I could make men die and bring them back to life. I could make them paupers or I could make them kings. No matter what the odds, my heroes could win, or die with honor.

I lower the drawbridge to childhood memories. I had to take naps in those days. I lay upon my bed gazing at yellow summer framed by the window. Shafts of light struck out across the room, particles of dust whirling about in them, riding invisible currents until they drifted off into the shadows. In each speck I saw a whole world. Years later I would hear of atoms, too small to be seen by men. A galaxy might be an electron in a more immense world. Nothing was beyond possibility. If it could be imagined, it lived. Creations of the mind are not bound by physical laws.

Physical creation is. I would like to bury my fear, but it is difficult when there is no activity with which to cover it. I must conserve as much energy as I can if I am to live. Every movement burns more fuel in my body's furnace. Steam rises from my dry skin. I tend the still and watch for ships. I will fish again when the time is right and the probability for success is high. The remaining time I sit quietly and try to divert my mind. I work on design ideas for boats and life rafts that I will complete in my warm, dry office when I return to Maine. Notes on safety systems, cruising boats, business and personal goals, all begin to find their way into my log. I often think of myself as a broker in the futures market.

I find some reassurance in contemplating multileveled reality. Last night's hot whole-wheat biscuits were almost as good as the real thing. I'm getting to love dreaming of food, rather than hating its tempting vision. Dreaming is the closest I can get to it, and being close to nourishment and drink is better than nothing.

I have become both the real and the dream. I now see many worlds surrounding me: the past, present, and future; the conscious and unconscious; the tangible and the imagined. I try to convince myself that it is only the present that is hellish, that all of the other worlds are untouchable, securely unimprison-able. I want desperately to keep these other worlds safe from pain and depression so that I can escape to them whenever I wish. My own propaganda is intoxicating, but I know reality's sharp, penetrating, dominating qualities. Steven Callahan is not free to leave. Today things flow smoothly, but tomorrow waves may break, crush my spirit, and wash away my dreams.

As the sky darkens and dusk sweeps across the water, they come. My feet, butt, and arms are beaten, as if I'm being mauled by a gang of hoodlums. For a time I drive the dorados off with a spear, but they always return. Time and again they strike, more and more joining in.

They have come for me. If I fall into the water, my doggies will devour me. Visions of Hitchcock's *The Birds* flash into my mind. Perhaps the fish of the world have held council, have condemned man's insatiable appetite and exploitation of the sea. Man has justified it by calling it utilization of resources by a superior species. The fish have lost patience with his egotism. I envision sailors' skeletons picked clean, their vacant eye sockets gazing up toward the flickering surface as they sink into the dark depths. Why do the dorados do this? Why are they in such a frenzy? How can simple fish be so frightening?

The blanket of night is pulled across the world. Sleep comes to the fish. I can see the school, between thirty and forty dorados, gently pacing the raft. They glow like silver platters on black velvet. Some shimmer up at me, beckoning, from several fathoms below. They await the light, the next round at dawn, and a day's hunt for flying fish. I close my eyes and drift into other places.

Whack! A tremendous blow to my back. Snapping slaps race across the floor of the raft like machine-gun fire. The raft leaps completely off the water with a twisted-rubber squeal and crashes back down. Shark attack! I spring to the entrance with weapon in hand. The slapping was a dorado; the shark must have pinned it under the floor. Now he forgets the fish, grabs the raft, and jerks it about by one of the ballast pockets on the other side. I can't get to him without risking falling overboard. Wait, you must wait. A raspy blow comes from port. Wait, got to wait. It's as black as hell out, I can't see anything. There it is. I jab—hit! He thrusts away, turns, attacks. Another blow knocks me off my knees. I wait—damn! He rakes across the bottom toward me. Jab—hit! Again the water swirls and explodes as he turns and knocks me down. Bastard! Wait . . . Darkness, stillness. I'm trembling all over; I reach for my water bottle and take a few swigs. For an hour each little slap of water or groan of rubber causes me to jump, ready to fend off a new attack. To be out of this . . . If only . . .

Was it only half a day ago that I felt so confident, that I convinced myself that reality was just a small part of my life and that my imagination could give me security? Now it seems that rows of razor teeth and deep, searing sores are all that there is, and I cannot escape from this dismal keep, even in dreams. How slim my chances *really* are. Perhaps I should simply give up rather than continue this pointless struggle.

I fight the vision of fourteen hundred miles of wet desert separating me from the first oasis. I try to forget my fear of the attacks. I struggle with my weariness of pumping up the raft and divert my nerves from the caustic cuts on my back and knees. Exhausted, I find sleep for another hour.

My dreams are broken again by a dorado flapping outside. Grabbing my gun, I rip open the tent flap. There is no attack. The water lies still. My eye catches sparkling lights on the black horizon. A ship!

She looks to be traveling across my bow, maybe four miles off. I rummage for my flares and gun. I drop in one of the fat red babies and clink the chamber closed. I whisper to her, "Do good by me now," stand, point the wide barrel to the heavens, and let her rip. An orange sun pops into the sky, belches smoke, and softly illuminates a small parachute as it dangles toward the sea. Swinging in its gentle descent, its light falls as a halo over the bleak waters two hundred feet below.

The lights of the ship are at a closer angle. I whoop and

holler. "She's seen me!" I wait and then let flare number two fly. My spirits blaze with the light. My weak legs begin to dance. I watch the ship approach. No more sharks! Home! Fresh dorado, queen of the seas, to the crew! I duck inside and begin throwing my knife, water, and goodies into the sack. The ship may leave my raft behind. I at least want my equipment: the only physical things I have left in the world. What a relief to forget about sipping water. I take several healthy swallows as I glance out.

A fine mist is coming down. The ship is approaching a little to the south of me. Glowing ports and a brightly lit bridge emanate warmth and companionship. Saved! Fourteen days and I'm saved! I fire a third flare. "I'm up here," I yell. Visions of my rescue race into my mind . . .

"Where are you bound?" the trim-bearded captain asks.

"Looks like wherever you are."

"Ha, I guess that's true enough! Gibraltar is our next stop."

I present him with the strings of fish. "Sorry to have chopped them up like this. Had I known you were going to pop by for dinner, I'd have sliced them into proper steaks."

"I've got duties to attend to. You get some rest, and I'll see you on the bridge when you feel up to it."

"I should recover fast. I was in pretty good shape before I left." *I pause and reflect. "I've been damned lucky haven't I? Haven't I? . . ."*

The fantasy recedes as I fire off a hand flare. My immediate world is lit up like day. My fish escort can be easily seen through the water. Their bodies smoothly undulate, seemingly oblivious to the idea that their companion will soon disappear. With such a flat sea, perfect visibility, and the ship only a mile off, the watch couldn't miss seeing me.

The ship's bow continues to cut purposefully toward the lightening dawn. Her wake is highlighted as it sweeps astern under her escaping cabin lights. A smooth, roiling path, the rumble of engines, and a plume of smoke trail behind. The mist is heavy now, almost a light rain. My excited heart has been pounding off the cold. Now the sagging of my enthusiasm allows this chill to creep under my skin. Dark bands of clouds are lit by the rising sun just under the horizon. I set off another hand flare, still confident that I have been seen. Wakes from the ship rock the raft, and I ride them out still standing. He'll turn and approach to windward. As the flare dies, a tall burning ember, like a devil's fire cone, stands in my hand. I throw it down, smoking and sizzling as it hits the surface, then groaning and boiling as it sinks into the depths.

There is a faint smell of diesel in the air. Perhaps I have a last chance. Someone may be on the afterdeck. I fire a fourth parachute flare. Then I collapse. She's missed me.

Fool, fool, damn fool! You have wasted six flares, count 'em, six, you turkey! The water bottle shows that you have downed a pint of hard-won stock. You were cocky; you were wasteful; you confused dreams with reality.

A light, frigid shower falls upon my body as I stand and watch the horizon until only a wisp of smoke can be seen. I should have realized that I wouldn't be saved by the first ship to pass my way. The Baileys had to wait until the eighth. It is not good business to bank on a check that is supposedly in the mail. I will be saved only when I feel the steel of a deck under my feet.

Dougal Robertson said not to count on shipping: "Rescue will come as a welcome interruption of . . . the survival voyage." Typical bloody British understatement! Ranting and raving is my style! After a few minutes, my Irish fire is as cooled and drowned as the dead flare, now a mile below me.

Things could be worse, I suppose. Perhaps he did see me and will radio for air assistance. I flip on the EPIRB. I doubt an aircraft will arrive, but I may be   FEBRUARY 19 closer to shipping than I expected. My spirits   DAY 15 are good enough to be cynical, even if I'm not smiling. I chide myself—no coffee for this morning's breakfast; dreadful state of affairs.

Will rescue come before another shark attack? Hopes. Hopes. But I face the reality that I will probably have to battle with more sharks. Since losing *Solo,* I have tried to save my energy, but the thoughts that bounce around in my brain are wearing me down. I'm too aware of how full of clichés my thoughts seem to be, the clichés one would expect from a struggling survivor. There are the promises to the cosmos that if only I am let out of this mess, I'll surely be good from now on. There are the constant dreams of food and drink, the aching loneliness, the fear. How I would like to take command of my situation, to entertain myself with enlightened thought, to heroically forget pain and fear, to keep control. Perhaps that kind of heroism exists only in novels. If there is any enlightenment that I have been awakened to, it is that men's minds are dominated by their little aches and pains. We want to think that we are more than that, that we control our lives with our intellect. But now, without civilization clouding the issue, I wonder to what extent intellect is controlled by instinct and culture is the result of raw gut reactions to life. I was brought up with the idea that I could do anything, be anything, survive anything. I want to believe it, try to believe it.

As I nibble my morning meal on the fifteenth day, the battle with the dorados begins again. Their powerful jaws snap at my hands and feet. I try to curl up on my cushion to soften the blows, and occasionally I drive them off. As daylight fills the sky, they dart off to hunt, returning every now and then to group with others and butt the raft. Flying fish burst from the water in the distance. They skitter for a hundred yards or more, weaving this way and that, their wings banking to the turns and their tails flickering like little propellers. Dorados race off and leap after the flyers, their favorite prey, or they shoot out of the waves in high arcs just for the fun of it. At sunset they return as if my raft is the school's rendezvous point.

I'm continually faced with hard decisions. Each time I fish, I risk damaging the spear gun and the raft. If that happens and

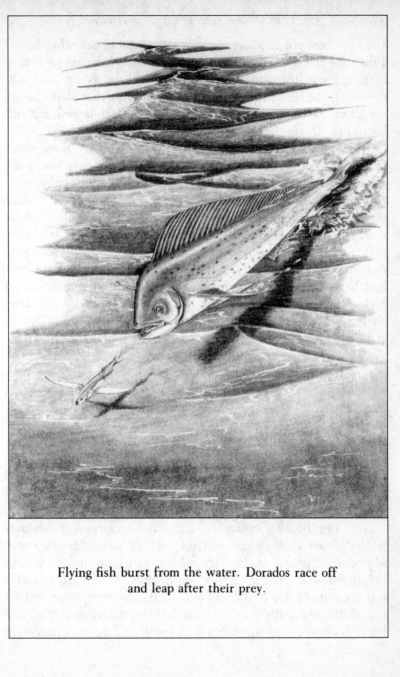

Flying fish burst from the water. Dorados race off
and leap after their prey.

I am not rescued in short order, I may die. On the other hand, I may die if I don't fish enough. Every time I decide on taking action, I run through the possible results to try to rationally decide on the best thing to do, but I am finding that all decisions are a two-edged sword, that any action may both benefit me and harm me. In the final analysis, everything is a gamble.

During their attacks, I have speared ten dorados. Some meat from the first dorado I caught still hangs in the butcher shop. I don't want to kill them needlessly; I wish that they could intuit this and leave me alone. They attack at dawn and dusk. I spear two of them securely and pluck them from the water. Their eyes meet mine as I hold their kicking bodies away from the raft. Frustrated, I yell at them. "There, is that what you want, stupid fish?" They tear free, ripping large holes in their fins and back. It does not seem to faze them. They return. I can feel a small tear in one of the ballast pockets, and I fear that the fish will not stop until they have destroyed me. I try to convince myself that their attacks are more pragmatic, that they are after the barnacles under me.

Growing on the bottom of the raft are the beginnings of goose-neck barnacles, so named for the long, tough stalks from which hang their lumpy black bodies. The adults are armored with bright white yellow-rimmed multiple shell plates that fit together like a puzzle. The baby barnacles on the raft are only about one-third of an inch long and have no hard shells. Once, *Napoleon Solo* was heeled over on the same tack for two weeks. Even though *Solo* sailed like a wizard, a farm of barnacles sprouted on the smooth paint underwater above her antifouling.

Anything floating in the sea is an island. Flotsam allows barnacles and weeds to grow. These act as nurseries for many animals and plants and attract small fish, which in turn attract larger fish—including sharks—and birds. When Chris and I left the Azores, we found an eight-inch cube of styrofoam floating in the sea with a fourteen-inch fish parked under it. We lifted its home and the fish swam about in circles, completely

Anything floating in the sea is an island. Triggerfish eat goose-
neck barnacles on a piece of flotsam and investigate
some sargasso weed in the background.

confused. We picked up fishing floats and lines cast adrift for some months. Every inch of floating paraphernalia housed a cluster of barnacles two inches long, as well as crabs, fish, worms, and shrimp. I've seen a mere strand of weed that had been swept out into the Gulf Stream accompanied by reef fish that had drifted with it over a thousand miles from their home. My raft and I are a large island by comparison.

It is heartening to see the ecology develop. Meat, especially the fish sticks of dorado, is very high in protein, but most vitamins are found in photosynthesizing organisms. Plants and the animals that feed on them, such as barnacles and triggerfish, yield more vitamins than the meat of the carnivorous dorados. Organ meats are also higher in vitamins, because they process the food that the fish digest. Experiments have shown that even without any vitamin C, a person shouldn't get scurvy for forty days, but any number of diseases or organ failures can result from lack of other vitamins. I hope the barnacles, triggers, and fish organs will provide enough. The line that trails to the man-overboard pole is made of twisted strands, with long, spiraled furrows that make a good field for barnacle growth. But every good thing has a price. The growth feeds me but slows me down, and the developing food chain will attract sharks.

In addition to the little ecosystem developing around my raft, I am constantly surrounded by a display of natural wonders. The acrobatic dorados perform beneath ballets of fluffy white clouds. The clouds glide across the sky until they join at the horizon to form whirling, flaming sunsets that are slowly doused by nightfall. Then, as if the sun had suddenly crashed, thousands of glistening galaxies are flung out into deep black night. There is no bigger sky country than the sea. But I cannot enjoy the incredible beauty around me. It lies beyond my grasp, taunting me. Knowing it can be stolen from me at any time, by a dorado or shark attack or by a deflating raft, I cannot relax and appreciate it. It is beauty surrounded by ugly fear. I write in my log that it is a view of heaven from a seat in hell.

My mood follows the sun. The light of each day makes me optimistic that I might last another forty, but the darkness of each night makes me realize that, if any one thing goes wrong, I will not survive. My rapidly shifting moods chase one another until I feel completely confused. Writing helps to keep things in perspective, but I wish for a companion who could tell me if I am dreaming or even sane. If I crack, I may waste my flares, or worse.

My wandering mind often stumbles upon words from what seems like lifetimes ago. Fragmentary pieces of my past fall snugly into place to form a pattern and give depth to things that at the time were merely whimsical. My mother and I were speaking of the dangers of singlehanded sailing. "No, I only wear a harness if it's too nasty out to trust my hold on the ship," I said. "The thing gets in the way, gives me something else to get tangled in or to trip over—right over the side." "You should at least wear a life jacket," she scolded. "If I *do* go over and watch my boat sail off into the sunset," I told her, "I don't relish the idea of hanging about for several days while my flesh is slowly picked by fish, like some kind of oceanic bird feeder." She was not amused and harrumphed. "After all the trouble I had in giving you life, you had better not give up that easily." Her words haunt me. "You have to promise me to hang on as long as you can." It was a promise never made, but it is being kept just the same.

Not long before I left *Solo* behind, I read a Robert Ruark novel, *Poor No More*. The grandfather spoke to the book's hero when he was a boy, something like, "Look, I know I'm goin' to die soon. Let's not make a big fuss about it. It don't matter. But look at your father. He never took one chance in his life and look at where it's gotten him. Don't you do that. Have the balls to kick life around a little bit. Make it hop!" My legs are too weak and wobbly to kick life around. I've taken those chances and where have they taken me? This vagabond is bushed. Still, I must try to keep on course until a safe anchorage is reached.

When I was sixteen I lay in bed with blood poisoning in my foot. Instead of dwelling on my ailment, I told myself that at least I still had a clear head, strong arms, and one good leg.

About me lie the remnants of *Solo*. My equipment is properly secured, vital systems are functioning, and daily priorities are set, priorities not to be argued with. I somehow rise above mutinous apprehension, fear, and pain. I am captain of my tiny ship in treacherous waters. I escaped the confused turmoil following *Solo*'s loss, and I have finally gotten food and water. I have overcome almost certain death. I now have a choice: to pilot myself to a new life or to give up and watch myself die. I choose to kick as long as I can.

High noon. The sun sizzling overhead roasts my dry skin. I sponge seawater onto my torso and let small pools collect in its hollows until they disappear. Resting on one side to let my back and upper side heal, I envision myself sprawled on an Antiguan beach. In a moment I will arise and fetch a cold rum punch— no need to yet, plenty of time.

Strips of fish have been drying on the canopy. Thin layers of fat under the skin glisten in the sun. The outsides are dried to a bronze color. They are slightly salty and spicy, rivaling the best sausage.

Things seem to be improving. For two and one half days there have been no shark raids. The morning and evening attacks of the dorados have been less ferocious—either that, or I'm noticing them less. A shower broke yesterday's heat. I opened my mouth as I did when I was a child trying to catch snowflakes. The rain wet my face, and I trapped another six ounces in my Tupperware box. I have begun to rebuild my water stock. When I first saw the squall approaching, I pulled up the painter astern and let the precipitation wash the barnacles clean. With my knife I easily peeled three or four ounces of barnacles from the line. Mixed with rainwater, they made a slightly crunchy soup, which I drank from my Tupperware box. I couldn't get the idea of a McDonald's Quarter-Pounder McBarnacle

FEBRUARY 21
DAY 17

Burger out of my mind. Soaked with salt water in a plastic bag, the remaining raisins had fermented until they bore little resemblance to the original fruit. But they made a final treat for my banquet—they were my last food from terra firma.

Grinding hunger is not what plagues me now. It is slow starvation. My body knows what it needs. For hours on end fantasies of sweet ice cream, starchy baked bread, and vitamin-rich fruits and vegetables water the mouth in my mind, though my real mouth long ago gave up its vain attempts to salivate. Not an evening passes without dreams of food.

When I feel confident, I dream of the future. My friends are building homes. We carry long timbers and heave them into place. We stop to lunch from tables piled high with bread and fruit. Often I fantasize about opening an inn in Maine where good food will be served—sherried crab in flaky pie shells, chocolate pies, cold beer. We eat slowly, calmly, overlooking the placid indigo waters of Frenchman Bay, where mountains stubbornly shoulder the cold Atlantic.

I pool my energies to tend my equipment. I lash mirrors and a small strobe light to the man-overboard pole; I tie up the leaky observation port on the canopy. My navigation puts me about one-fifth of the way to the Caribbean Islands. It's a sobering realization. Can I last another sixty days? My mind turns to the unbearable suffering the Baileys must have known. I cannot imagine over a hundred days of this. But then, what of those whose whole lives are spent in starvation?

I envision my own end coming at any moment with the snap of jaws, but somehow I feel fated to survive. I lost everything I owned with *Solo,* but it is intriguing to think of what it will be like to start over again with no worldly goods, with only experience.

On calm days I can move my weight away from the windward side without fear of capsizing. I sit across from the butcher shop where my fish hang from their clotheslines. This is the one spot in the raft where I can sit almost upright. From here I can easily tend the still every half hour, watch part of the horizon, write, and navigate. Time and again I plot my possible position. Sixty days . . . It seems impossible, but many things that are hard to believe do happen.

George Bracy is a friend of mine back in Maine. He's one of the old-timers, a lobsterman and clammer in his younger days. Some folks call him the Geezer. Like most men of the sea, George can spin any number of wild and barely believable yarns. There is the one about the time he roller-skated down Cadillac Mountain, back when clumsy steel wheels were advanced technology. Or the one about the man he saw who jumped from a height of a thousand feet without a parachute onto a mattress below, wearing only a jumpsuit with flaps of cloth between the legs and arms. By the time I knew him, George was slowed by arthritis. "Was paralyzed from the waist down for twelve yea's. Doctors said I'd always be that way. Then, one day I was sittin' on a log cuttin' up some stove wood when I fell off, and lo and behold, I could walk just fine."

It's hard to tell when men are remembering things as they were and when they have innocently constructed or elaborated on memories. But every now and then the Geezer would surprise the skeptical. You might get a glimpse of an old newspaper clipping titled, "Local Lobsterman G. Bracy Roller-skates down Cadillac," or spy an old photo of a barnstorming acrobat clothed only in a baggy jumpsuit, with the caption, "Calls himself the Batman." Who is to say what is not true and what is not possible?

Ship ho! I glance up and there she is, close by, a sweetly lined red-hulled freighter with white whale strake and shapely bow slicing her way right for me. It's incredible that I haven't seen her sooner. They must have spotted the raft and are headed over to check it out. I load the flare pistol to satisfy their curiosity. As it shoots skyward and pops, the vessel cuts the distance between us at twelve to fourteen knots. The flare isn't as bright as it would be at night, but the crew can't miss its smoke and flame hanging in the air. If anyone is looking, it is impossible for him not to see me. The raft isn't disappearing into any troughs, and I have the full ship continually in view. I light an orange smoke flare that hisses and wafts a tawny genie downwind, close to the water. My eyes search the bridge and deck for signs of life. The ship is now so close that if a deckhand scurries into view I will be able to tell what he is wearing. But the only thing moving is the ship itself. I pull in the man-overboard pole, extend it high over my head, and wave frantically. I shriek above the soft murmur of the raft gliding over the water, the shush of the ship's bow wave, and the beat of her engine. "Yeoh! Here! Here! Bloody hell can't you see!" I yell as loud as I can until my throat cracks. I know that my voice must be drowned out by shipboard clamor. Still, it is a relief to break the silence. She steams on. Such a lovely ship . . . too bad. Within twenty minutes she has disappeared over the horizon.

How many others can possibly pass so close? Most likely none. How many will pass that I will not see? How many won't see me? In this century there are few eyes aboard ships. In heavily traveled sea lanes, where collison is an immediate threat, a good watch is kept. Navy ships also have the manpower and the desire to keep a constant lookout. But in the open ocean, the captain of a merchant ship may keep only one of his few crew on the bridge to take a cursory glance about the horizon every now and then. *Maybe* there's an eye on the radar. *Maybe* the VHF radio is flipped on to channel 16 while the vessel charges blindly over the ocean under the automatic pilot's command. And even if there is a watch, after seeing that no ships are in view he turns his attention back to his novel or girly magazine, or he steps out onto the bridge to take a smoke in the shade. My raft would be hard to spot even if a ship had been notified. A 250-foot red freighter didn't appear to my eyes until it was almost upon me. What chance does my bubble have of being seen? Perhaps I should stay awake at night when flares are most effective. But I must stay awake in the day to properly tend the still. And a good watch at night would cut my precious water supply. I try to calm my frustrations by repeating, "You are doing the best you can. You can only do the best you can." One thing is clear. I cannot rely on others to save me. I must save myself.

The freedom of the sea lures men, yet freedom does not come free. Its cost is the loss of the security of life on land. When a storm is brewing, the sailor cannot simply park his ship and walk away from it. He cannot hide within stone walls until the whole thing blows over. There is no freedom from nature, the power that binds even the dead together. Sailors are exposed to nature's beauty and her ugliness more intensely than most men ashore. I have chosen the sailor's life to escape society's restrictions and I have sacrificed its protection. I have chosen freedom and have paid the price.

The last wisp of smoke lies faint on the horizon where the ship disappeared. Despite my rationalization, I am bitterly disappointed. I am not angry, but I am ready to be enslaved by shoreside life for a while. Words of *The Old Man and the Sea* come to me. "If only the boy were here . . . if only the boy." I need a rest, another set of eyes, the companionship of another voice. But even a companion would not improve my chances. There would not be enough water for two of us.

Perhaps flying a kite will increase my visibility. I cut a swatch from the space blanket and make a diamond-shaped bird, using a couple of battens from the piece of mains'l as a cross frame. It's pretty heavy for its size and needs a tail. I can't get it to fly from the raft, but maybe I can perfect it by the time I get to the shipping lanes. It is quite effective as a water gutter. I tie it up to the back of the tent, where it catches most of the spray that dribbles through the observation port. A proper kite would be a valuable piece of emergency equipment, a bright beacon flying hundreds of feet above the ocean, but mine is destined to assist in keeping things dry, which helps me heal.

Again the sun sets, the fish attack. I pump up the raft's slowly deflating tubes, eat my fish sticks, search for rest and find only sleep. Again in the night a shark comes. It rips across the bottom with astounding speed and tears me from comfortable fantasy.

As it scrapes under a second time, I strain to detect its form in the depths but cannot. It is gone, and for another windless night the raft flops and awaits the final attack.

Until now I have referred to my raft simply as "the raft." I decide that it must have a name. I have owned two inflatable dinghies in the past, and I jokingly named them *Rubber Ducky I* and *Rubber Ducky II*. It only makes sense to continue the tradition. Therefore, I dub thee *Rubber Ducky III*.

In the morning I crawl around on top of *Rubber Ducky,* sliding my hands over the rubber, feeling for signs of deterioration. The bottom feels good, at least as far under as I can reach, but there are several divots in the bottom tube around the gas cylinder. Perhaps they've been there all along, or perhaps a shark has been chewing on my raft. The gas cylinder hanging under the raft still worries me, but I can't think of anything to do about it.

Above the water, the tubes are beginning to road-map with cracks from the baking sun. The exterior handline is so tight in spots that it chafes on the tubes. When the raft was tied to *Solo,* the force from the sea's attack must have yanked it through the anchoring points. With all my might, I try to loosen and readjust it, with no effect. The orange-pigmented waterproofing of the canopy has been bleached, beaten, and washed off. It no longer keeps water out of the raft, and any rainwater picks up small orange particles. Trying to swallow it is like forcing down another man's vomit. If I could have effectively collected water from the past showers, I'd be about six pints richer. I curse it. Robertson says that one can absorb up to a pint of undrinkable fresh water by enema, but I have no way to give myself one.

The sun rises and the bake-off begins again. My past continues its procession before my mind's eye. There is no freedom to get on with my future. I am not dying and I am not finding salvation. I am in limbo.

In my mind, a cool stream winds through tall verdant trees. I look into the bubbling water as it tumbles over a rocky bottom.

The smell of fresh biscuits wound around sticks, browning over a campfire, fills my nostrils. It is really just the smell of drying fish.

I see a majestic harbor full of yachts. *Solo* is there. The ragged volcanic peaks of Madeira rise in my mind. Eons ago they grew from the sea bottom and blasted out upon the surface. Catherine and I ride the bus that rattles its way around the torn precipices, on cobbled, snaking roadways carved into the vertical slopes. Villages that are a few miles apart by air are an hour apart by road. A gentle toss will carry a stone thousands of feet down. It takes eight hours to drive thirty miles. Lush, terraced fields stretch from oceanside valleys up the slopes until they reach vertical rock. Farmers harvest grapes, for famous Madeira wine, bananas, and other fruits of every variety, including some found only on this mystical isle. We investigate a village perched high upon a ridge over the sea. Melodies from Catherine's flute intertwine with a northerly breeze that sweeps up the slopes, bringing with it the music of crashing surf. Elegant peaks, soft valleys, and tranquil people combine in a fairy tale setting.

It is Sunday. There is no electricity. No TV football, no video games. The people of the village line the street, occasionally shifting positions with their neighbors to gossip or simply to look on while life passes by. The island's natural wealth allows this tranquility. Water springs everywhere. I want a beer. *"Aberto, senhor?"* He is not supposed to be open, but we are special. The bar is the basement of an ancient house. Its damp rock walls cool us. A tap pokes out from one wall. A large wooden cask sits dimly lit in the back. Spiced tomato sauce filled with tender beef boils atop a corner stove. The man gives us beer and fills glasses with wine from the cask. It's new wine from his vineyard. He hands me a sandwich of the spiced meat, too. He welcomes us into his life as if we are old friends, but we do not stay. I must get on to the Canaries.

We originally planned a two-week voyage, but winds have been light. Catherine and I have been together for over a month.

She is a good crew, eager to learn, but she expects more. She expects all men to love her. It is an odd turnabout from the usual female complaint: "All my captain wants to do is get me into the sack." To Catherine I am aloof and silent. "You are a hard man," she continually tells me.

It is probably true. Most of the women I've been close to have been very liberated types. I have always respected that, but in turn I've demanded much from them. I have demanded that I should not be subjected to female chauvinism, that I should not be duty bound to do all of the "man's work." So when Catherine has been on watch and a jib or pole has fouled and she has implored me for help, I have snapped at her, "When it is your watch, *you* deal with it!" But I know that my hardness is more than this. My impatience and unkindness stem from deeper roots. Seven years of marriage ending in divorce—and an ensuing hot relationship that left me singed—have made me tired of the traumas of women and of love. Perhaps it is a fear that I am unwilling to face. Perhaps I have traded my quest for love for the quest to finish what I set out to do. I don't really know, but these are among the secrets that I'm unwilling to share with Catherine, despite her soft French voice and lovable smiles. I only want to sail, write, and draw. If anything, as our voyage lengthens, the more she tries to soften me up, the harder I become. I want my boat back to myself. As if I am afraid of the magic that the tranquility of Madeira is spinning, I set sail after only three days. Was I wrong? Safe harbors . . . that is what I want *now*. Why did I push on? Why did I not allow myself to soften?

I'm determined to taste campfire biscuits again, to feel cool streams; I will build another ship and give myself another chance to feel the warmth of human passion. I do not think "if I get home" but only "when I get home."

I was foolish to let those dorados escape. The butcher shop is bare. My stomach churns and growls in anguish. I hunt my companions for days on end. I begin to recognize many. One

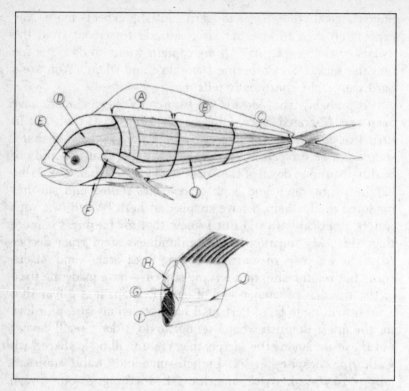

still trails a fishing line from its mouth, another has a torn fin, another a large gash in its back that is slowly scarring over. There are differences in size and slight variations in color. The females differ markedly from the males. They are slimmer, smaller, with more rounded foreheads. I often see two very distinctive bright green fish that never approach closely. The female is over four feet long, the male even bigger. Dorados up to six feet long, weighing sixty pounds, have been recorded. The emerald elders are as wary of me as I am of them. The youngsters ignore their warnings and come close to the raft, still cautious. They know where I can shoot, and they avoid these areas or sneak by when I'm not looking. They slowly swim into range and then dart this way or that. These fish are not stupid,

Cleaning the dorados has become more thorough and pristine. After removing the organs from the organ cavity (I), the body is divided into segments (A, B, C), head, and tail. The segments can be cut into strips and hung up to dry. The muscle fibers run the length of the fish and become more tendinous at the tail. The tastiest and most tender steaks are cut from the back, above the lateral line (J), and closest to the head. A couple of steaks for immediate consumption may be cut from section A across the muscle fibers. All others must be cut lengthwise so they can be hung without falling apart. The organ cavity (I) ends at about mid-section (B). Aft of this, sticks can be cut below the lateral line (J) as well as above it. In the cross section, the backbone (G) and the bones that support the fin divide the body into quadrants, which are cut off of the bones before the flesh is sliced into sticks. A small amount of fat is found in belly steaks and in the meat attached to the pelvic and pectoral fins (F); I call this my fried chicken. A steak (D) can be cut from the side of the head. The eyes with their associated muscles and fatty fluids (E) provide moisture. The eyes, small bits of meat scraped off the head, organs, and a couple of steaks provide the first meal. The backbone, ribs lining the organ cavity, and fins are saved along with the fish sticks for later meals.

and they can swim at fifty knots, making them the fastest fish alive. The emerald elders leap yards through the air and land with a thunderous slap. I would not be surprised to see them suddenly take off in flight. It is as if their play is a statement to me: "Behold the magnificence that our race can attain." Yet these fish are modest creatures. They say nothing and swim on.

Finally I manage to spear a triggerfish. The tiny fillets are little comfort, but she is full of sweet eggs. My body seems to immediately revive from the nutrients. A third ship approaches, but farther off. I fire a flare. It passes. I now have only two meteor, two smoke, and two parachute flares left. The ships have been eastbound, three or four days apart. I must be near the lanes. Perhaps I'll be lucky the fourth time.

It is February 26, my twenty-second day adrift. I cannot complain too much as the morning has been relatively good. The raft is moving well, the sun is out. My second dorado lies slain before me. My cleaning of the dorados has become more thorough. I don't waste anything. I eat the heart and liver, suck the fluid from the eyes, and break the backbone to get the gelatinous nuggets from between the vertebrae. I have rationed myself only a half pint of drinking water per day, so I have built up my stock to six and a half pints. I am clear-headed, and the raft is holding up. I am feeling O.K., but I am very conscious that my spirits fall and rise with the undulating waves.

FEBRUARY 26
DAY 22

Then the afternoon sun focuses on me. Magnified as if through a glass, it seems to burn holes in my chest. I struggle to my knees in order to tend the still and look around. Dizziness overtakes me, nearly knocking me over as darkness closes in on the edges of my vision. All is blue and hazy as I fumble for the coffee can and pour water over my scalp. I collapse, vaguely seeing waves press ahead to my destination.

Like a thunderclap, the windward side of the raft crushes in upon me, flips forward, and the bow digs into the sea. Water pours in. This is it—capsize, I think calmly, but the stern pops back into shape and flops down. About twenty gallons of water slosh around me. My sleeping bag, some notes, the cushion, and other gear float about. The rogue wave melts into the distance ahead, a messenger signaling that worse is to follow.

The flooding has revived me from catatonic lethargy. Mechanically I set to the exhausting work of bailing and wringing out. Another three days of cold, wet gear. My sleeping bag is already a bundle of knots and lumps, encrusted with salt when dry. It is hard work just to wring out most of the water and get the bag to the merely wet stage. In the ensuing evenings, the crinkly, clammy space blanket will provide my best cover. My scabs have been torn off again. The suddenness of these sieges by the sea and its creatures gives me no quarter.

I stand, face the growing wind and seas, and support my wobbly legs by holding on to the canopy. Waves jostle my platform and gurgle about my feet. Cirrus clouds mat the sky like shaggy white dog hair dropped from the heavens. Things are getting bleaker both inside and out.

I try to keep a positive perspective. The essentials—food, water, shelter—are being maintained. My mind is sometimes free to wander and to make my life more than the here and now. I am the past. I am what others have known and felt about me. I am the things I have done. These are my afterlife. These cannot be captured or killed. I know this is only temporary reassurance, but I am inspired enough to regularly get up off my cushion, feel the cold air against my skin, and survey my surroundings. I cannot afford to miss a passing ship.

I find a small hole in the second still, tape it up, and get it temporarily working again, continuing to build my water stock. No matter how positive I try to be, approaching scud and wind blow upon me the fear of another gale.

By morning the wind is whistling. The heaving sea raises ten-foot waves, which spew, curl, and crash down. I hang on to windward, wrapped in my salty sleeping bag. In quick darts to the downwind side, I tend to the solar still and snatch a glance about. Watch-keeping is a joke. The visible horizon is very close. I stand and balance as well as I can on the rubber floor, rising and falling with the waves. As the raft is elevated to the peak of a wave, I bend my knees to compensate for the liftoff. We hesitate for a moment on the top before plunging down into the trough. During this brief pause, my eyes sweep across a segment of the horizon. It takes a couple of minutes of rising and plummeting before I get a clear look all around. Every now and then I get a glimpse of something off to the north. But the massive, rolling shoulders and white foamy heads of waves crowd my view. Finally I'm lifted to the top of a big roller. Yes! There she is! A ship, northbound. Unfortunately, there's no

FEBRUARY 27
DAY 23

hope of her picking me up. She's pointed away from me and too distant to spot a flare. I am encouraged only by her direction —South Africa to New York. What was merely a dream twenty-four desperate days ago, I have made real. I have reached the lanes and I still live.

TO
WEAVE
A
WORLD

THE METAL IS HARD

and cold. After an hour of leaning over the bulwark, my elbows are in icy pain. I stand and thrust my hands deep into the wool coat the captain has brought me. "I'll bet you never thought you'd see this city again," he says, looking at me quizzically. I peruse the horizon. It is no longer flat and empty but is full of monolithic skyscrapers, gray smog. The noise of the city rises above even the rumble of reversed engines. Heavy, tattooed arms pull aboard hawsers as thick as thighs and whip them around the capstans. Slowly the ship is worked in to the dock. More and more lines are tossed and set. The water eddies around us. The behemoth is reeled in. No, I never thought I'd see New York again.

Then there is darkness and chaos. My head is struck with a club, cold, wet, and hard. The assaulter roars, rumbles, and rolls away into the night. I am on the dark side of the earth, a quarter world away from New York. The wind is up and so is the sea. *Rubber Ducky* lurches and crashes as if caught in a demolition derby. "Still here," I moan.

Each night, soft fabrics caress my skin, the smell of food fills my nostrils, and warm bodies surround me. Sometimes while wrapped in sleep I hear my conscious mind bark a warning: "Enjoy it while you can for you will soon awaken." I am used to the duality of it. Usually when I sail alone, the sounds of fluttering sails and waves, the motion of my boat rising and plunging, never leave me even as I hang in my bunk dreaming of faraway places. If a movement varies slightly or an unfamiliar noise slaps against my eardrum, I am immediately awakened. Yet last night's dream was almost too real. My life has become a composition of multilayered realities—daydreams, night dreams, and the seemingly endless physical struggle.

I keep trying to believe that all of these realities are equal.

Perhaps they are, in some ultimate sense, but it becomes increasingly obvious that in the survival world my physical self and my instincts are the ringmasters that whip all of my realities into place and control their motions. My dreams and daydreams are filled with images of what my body requires and of how to escape from this physical hell. Since I have gotten the still to work and have learned how to fish more efficiently, there has been little to do but save energy, wait, and dream. Slowly, though, I find I am becoming more starved and desperate. My equipment is deteriorating.

I must work harder and longer each day to weave a world in which I can live. Survival is the play and I want the leading role. The script sounds simple enough: hang on, ration food and water, fish, and tend the still. But each little nuance of my role takes on profound significance. If I keep watch too closely, I will tire and be no good for fishing, tending the still, or other essential tasks. Yet every moment that I don't have my eyes on the horizon is a moment when a ship may pass me. If I use both stills now, I may be able to quench my thirst and keep myself in better shape for keeping watch and doing jobs, but if they both wear out I will die of thirst. My mind applauds some of my performances while my body boos, and vice versa. It is a constant struggle to keep control, self-discipline, to maintain a course of action that will best ensure survival, because I can't be sure what that course is. Is my command making the right decisions? Might immediate gratification sometimes be the best course to follow even in the long run? More often than not, all I can tell myself is, "You're doing the best you can."

I need more fish, and the constant nudging I feel through the floor of the raft tells me that the dorados are around in sufficient numbers to make fishing a reasonable expenditure of energy. After several misfires, I finally skewer a dorado by the tail, but it doesn't slow him down much. He yanks the raft all over the place while I frantically try to hold on, wishing that I could train these fish to pull me in the direction I want to go.

He pulls free before I can get him aboard. Oh well, try again. I start to reset the spear gun—but the power strap is gone, now sinking through three miles of seawater! This could be real trouble.

It's my first major gear failure; but I've dealt with a lot of jury rigs before so I should be able to figure something out. It's always a challenge to try and repair an essential system with what one has at hand. In fact, I sometimes wonder if one of the major reasons for ocean racing and voyaging is to push one's self and one's boat just past the edge, watch things fail, and then somehow come up with a solution. In many ways, having a jury rig succeed is often more gratifying than making a pleasant and uneventful passage or even winning a race. Rising to the challenge is a common thread that runs through a vast wardrobe of sea stories. I've stuck back together masts, steering gear, boat hulls, and a host of smaller items. Although I don't have much to work with, repairing the spear should be relatively simple.

The important thing is to keep calm. The small details of the repair will determine its success or failure. As always, I can only afford success. Don't hurry. Make it right. You can fish tomorrow. The arrow and the gun handle are still intact. It is only the source of power that is missing. I put the arrow on the shaft of the handle in the normal manner, but I pull the arrow out through the plastic loop on the end of the handle shaft in order to lengthen the weapon as much as possible. I wind two long lashings around the arrow and shaft. I use the heavy cod-line, which is better than synthetic line because it shrinks when it is wetted and then dried, thereby tightening the lashings. The smooth arrow still rotates, so I add a third lashing, then I add frappings to the lashings. These are turns of the line around the lashings at right angles. When pulled tight, the frappings cinch up the lashings and should keep them from spreading out haphazardly. There are notches in the butt of the arrow, which normally fit into the trigger mechanism in the handle. Through these notches and back through the trigger housing, I pass loops of line to keep the arrow from being pulled out forward by an escaping fish.

I am aware that my repaired spear is a flimsy rig for catching dorados. Normally a diver pulls on his spear gun arrow when retrieving a fish. I must drive my lance through the fish, putting the rig in compression rather than tension. When I pull a fish out of the water, it will put a large bending load on the arrow as well. However, my new lance feels pretty sturdy, and I'm ready to try it out. Patience is going to be the secret, and strength. Power was stored in the elastic power strap; now the improvised spear has to be thrust at a moment's notice with all of the power I can muster if I'm to drive it through a thick dorado.

I lean my left elbow on the top tube of the raft to steady my aim, and I lightly rest the arrow of the spear between my fingers. I pull the gun handle high up onto my cheek with my right arm, tensed and steady, awaiting the perfect shot. I can sight down the shaft, and rocking back and forth gives me a narrow field of fire. On the water's surface is an imaginary circle about a foot in diameter into which I can shoot without moving my steadying elbow off the raft tube. If I am not well braced, my shots will become wild. The effective range of the spear has been shortened from about six feet to three or four. I must wait until a fish swims directly under my point so that it will be in range and the problem of surface refraction—which makes the fish appear to be where it is not—will be minimized. This problem is extreme at oblique angles to the water. When I shoot, I must extend my range and power as much as possible. I thrust my arm out straight and lunge as hard as I can with my whole body, trying to hold my aim. The shot must be instantaneous, because the fish are so quick and agile, but it also must be perfectly controlled. Once I lift my left, steadying arm off of the tube, it becomes hopeless. I watch the fish swimming all over the place, but I must wait for one to swim within my field of fire. I remain poised for minutes that stretch into hours at a time. I feel like I'm becoming an ancient bronze statue of a bowless archer.

I must remain poised for minutes that stretch
into hours at a time.

The doggies' nudging has become an advantage. I push my knees deeply into the floor just behind my arrow, luring them on. Bump, and a body slithers out, a little too far to starboard. Bump, a little too far to port. Head center! Do it! Splash! Strike! Ripping strong pull, white water, a cloud of blood. He's in the air. HUGE! A spray of blood. Ow! Feels like I'm being smashed by an oar as he slides down the spear toward me. Don't let go, get him in, quick! Fury flapping, blood flying. Watch the spear tip, the *tip, fool!* On the floor, onto him, now! The huge square-headed body lies still for a moment under my knee as I press my full weight down on him. His gills are puffing in rhythm with my gasps as I try to grasp the spear on both sides of his torso and give myself a moment's rest. A hole as big as my fist has been blasted out of his body, which stretches almost all the way across the floor. Globs of clotting blood swill about in the crater created by my other knee.

Whap, whap, whap! His thunderclapping tail smashes into action. I'm knocked over backward. He's escaped. The tip, watch the tip! He flops all round the raft, making for the exit. Pain in my wrist. Pain in my face. He's winning! I fumble for the tip of the spear as it whips about. Finally I tackle the fish, throw him down onto my sleeping bag and equipment sack, and bury the spear tip in the thick fabric. Both of us are panting. I can't reach my knife. His eye clicks around, calculating—little time left, and he knows it. Whap, whap, whap—he's off again. Look out! Fire shoots up my left arm. "Get down there, down!" Whap, whap, cracking around the raft like a bullwhip. Back on the bag again. Sprawled across him, pushing with my legs to get him pinned. Gills puffing. Get the knife. Push it in. Hits something hard—the spine. Twist it. Crack. Wait. He's still panting, slowly panting, stopped panting. Rest . . . I'll not do that again.

I can't believe that the raft hasn't been ripped. I examine the spear carefully; it is only slightly bent, and the lashings held. I listen but hear no hissing leaks. The tubes still feel hard. Blood and guts are spewed everywhere, some of it mine, no doubt. I'll try to stick to the smaller females in the future. Also from now on I will carefully arrange my equipment before beginning to fish. I'll stretch out the sailcloth across as much of the bottom as possible, put my cutting board down, and spread my sleeping bag over the tubes on the starboard half of the raft above my equipment sack. I have overcome the first serious gear failure since I coaxed the solar still to work.

For hours I slice up my grand fish. First I hack it into four large chunks, plus the head and tail. Then I slice each chunk into four long pieces, one from each side of the back and one from each side of the belly. Finally I slice these into sticks which I hang on strings to dry, like dozens of fat fingers, delicious fat fingers. I write in my log that this is a strange prison in which I am slowly starved but occasionally thrown a twenty-pound filet mignon.

The first weeks of my unplanned raft voyage have gone well—as well as can be expected. I escaped the immediate peril of *Solo*'s sinking, have adjusted to my equipment and the environment, and am now actually better stocked with food and water than when I began.

So much for the positive side. The negative is only too obvious. Lack of starches, sugars, and vitamins has let my body wither. My gluteus maximus was the first to go. Where my plump ass once was, there are only hollows of flesh ridged by pelvic bones. I try to stand as often and as long as possible, but my legs have badly atrophied and hang from my hips like threads with little knots for knees. There was a time when three hands could not encircle my thighs; now two will do, and nicely at that. My chest and arms have thinned but remain fairly strong due to the exercise demanded by survival. How the body steals heat or food from one part to lend to another, how it compensates for deprivation by shutting down all but the essential systems, how it possibly can keep this wreck running in this demo-derby of flesh, is all beyond me, amazing, almost amusing. I write in my log, "No more fat on this honky!"

The cuts on my knees still have not healed. Other gashes

have left thick scars. Dozens of small slits on my hands, made by my knife or fish bones, never seem to mend. Scar tissue builds up around the wounds like little volcanoes, leaving raw craters inside. Though I'm meticulous about sponging up water and keeping *Ducky* dry, I've spent about half of my time wet. The salt water sores begin as small, infected boils that grow, burst open, and leave ulcers penetrating the skin. These continue to widen and deepen, as if a slow-burning acid were being dropped on the flesh. But so far my work at keeping dry has paid off. I have only a dozen or two open sores, about a quarter inch across, clustered on my hips and ankles. My cushion and sleeping bag, when dry, are encrusted with salt, which grinds into my wounds.

MARCH 3
DAY 27

It is sunrise of the twenty-seventh day since I began my voyage in *Rubber Ducky III*. I roll and tie up the canopy's entry closure so its cold, wet skin won't lash across mine. I poke my head out, turn aft, and watch the rising sun as awestruck as a child witnessing it for the first time. I note its position relative to the raft.

Creases in *Ducky's* soft tubes open and close like toothless black mouths, munching on strings of glue and the white chalk markings of the raft inspectors. Sometimes I wonder who made these marks and what they are doing now. I hope that they are well, for they have done a good job and I am grateful. I push the pump hose into the hard white valves and begin my work, a job as thankless and never-ending as washing dishes and as tiring as a marathon. Ringed treads on the pump have worn thick callouses into my thumbs. The bellows utters a short, high-pitched whimper each time I squeeze it, like those baby dolls that cry out and weep tears. Uuh, uuh, uuh, uuh, one, two, three, four . . . uuh, uuh, uuh, uuh, fifty-seven, fifty-eight, fifty-nine, sixty. I pause, panting, feel the tube—not quite as firm as a watermelon yet—and continue. Then the bottom tube. Noontime, sunset, midnight, and morning, I squeeze the crying pump. In the early days, I had to listen to only sixty whimpers each day; now I have to squeeze over three hundred from the hateful little beast.

The still is sagging. Each morning I blow it up, empty the salt water from the distillate, and prime it. Then I get up to take a look around. Tricky. On a ship's solid deck the waves' motions are averaged out. Here my legs fall and rise with every ripple. Tiny bubbles and gurgles tickle the bottoms of my soft feet. Their callouses washed off long ago. I hang lightly on to the canopy, conscious that a hard tug may collapse it and drop me into the sea. Standing up in my vessel is a little like walking on water.

The only companions in sight are a petrel and a graceful shearwater. The petrel looks as out of place as I, fluttering like a sea chickadee, teetering on the edge of flight, heading straight for a clumsy crash. In reality he is having no trouble. I've seen petrels in shrieking winds, flapping from one gigantic wave canyon to another. They weigh only a few ounces and you'd think that they'd be blown off the face of the world. The tiny petrels, even the much larger shearwaters, will make a very meager meal, but I'll still try to grab one if it ventures close enough. Neither has any need for my dangerous company. They are only curious enough to swoop by every now and then. Their minute black eyes flit over every detail of the raft as they pass. I can watch the flight of the shearwaters for hours. They rarely flap their wings, even when it is flat calm. Then they glide in a straight line close to the surface of the water in order to use the surface effect. In heavy airs they wheel about in large arcs and then dive down so close to the waves that you can't see any space between their feather tips and the water. To me, they are the gods of grace. The shearwaters make me feel very clumsy and remind me how ill suited I am to this domain.

Robertson's book includes tables of the sun's declination, which I use to fix my direction at sunrise. I can do the same at sunset. At night I can fix my heading from both the North Star and Southern Cross. The heavens have provided me with an unbreakable, immortal, fully guaranteed compass. To measure my speed, I time the passage of seaweed between *Rubber Ducky* and the man-overboard pole. Earlier I had calculated the distance to the pole to be about seventy feet, or $1/90$ of a nautical mile. If it takes one minute for a piece of weed or other flotsam to pass between *Ducky* and the pole, I am going $60/90$ of a mile each hour, or $2/3$ of a knot, which works out to 16 miles a day. I make up a table for times from 25 to 100 seconds, $9\frac{1}{2}$ to 38 miles a day. I never do see a 38-mile day.

Since my chart shows the entire Atlantic Ocean on one sheet, my snail's-pace progress is hardly worth plotting on a daily basis, but every couple of days I plot another eighth or quarter inch. I kid myself that I only have a little ways left to travel—why, it's only about six inches on the map.

I am confident that we, that is *Ducky* and I, have reached the lanes and will soon be picked up, but we may well have drifted beyond them. I have tried the EPIRB again to no avail. The battery must be very low now. I must wait until I see positive signs of land or air traffic before I try it again. As soon as we arrived at what I thought to be the edge of the lanes, the wind strengthened. Perhaps Zephyrus wants to push us through before we can be spotted. I'm not too disappointed; it's a relief to be moving purposefully forward. There've been no sharks. There has also been only one ship in six days—pretty empty ocean highway.

Conditions are favorable for my tub. It's blowing hard enough to move us well, but not so hard that the waves are blasted apart. Unless we are hit by a rogue wave, *Ducky* will stay on her bottom. She slues down the slopes with a speedy motion that is smooth, quiet, and peaceful, seemingly frictionless. I get a vision in my head that I can't shake, one of a spaceship gliding in large curving banks through the vastness of space. In my log I sketch *Rubber Ducky* converted to a flying saucer with a wide band around her perimeter, studded with lights. I surround her with planets, stars, and fish.

Time for breakfast. I fall back on my cushion and lean up

against the equipment sack. I flip my sleeping bag over my legs, awaiting the warmth of the day. The fish sticks that have been hanging for two days are semidried and slightly chewy. Dorados begin their own daily routine, bumping my rear several times before flipping off to hunt.

Eight hard-won pints of water are carefully stored in three unopened water tins, two recapped and taped tins, two distillate plastic bags, and my working water jug. The butcher shop is chock-a-block full of fish sticks. Wet fresh protein is digested with less water than cooked or dried meat, so I try to eat a lot of my catch early on. As days pass and it gets chewier, I carefully ration the meat and begin fishing again.

I've become worried about my digestive tract. Dougal Robertson points to the case of one survivor who had no bowel movement for thirty days. By the time the body is through digesting the minuscule amount of food taken in, there simply is very little to move. I feel no urge to go but worry about a hemorrhoid that has puffed out. Should my plumbing suddenly blast loose, I may be in for a rupture and hemorrhage, which would be difficult to plug up and heal. I begin modified yoga exercises—twisting, bending, arching, stretching—slowly learning how to balance and compensate for the motion of my waterbed. On the thirty-first day, the bloody bubble begins to subside and a small amount of diarrhea relieves my apprehension.

Early morning, dusk, and night are the only times that I can coerce my body to exercise. By noon the temperature has rocketed to ninety degrees or more. It might as well be nine hundred. My body has no water to sweat. The air trapped inside of the raft is humid and stagnant. Staying conscious and tending the solar stills are major struggles. My spinning head coaxes me. Must get up, look around. Slow, easy now, to your knees. I gaze into the lively blue water. O.K. Wait now, maybe a few minutes. I try to get my eyes to focus, but they stumble about in my head, smash into the sides of my skull, and bounce back.

Grab the can, careful not to drop it, already lost one. I dip it down with a gurgle, raise it above me, and let the water fall, massaging my neck and tangled hair with cool relief. Again I dip the can, again and again, imagining that I'm crawling into shaded tall wet grass under a billowing willow tree.

Slowly now, lift your head. Look right. Look left. O.K. Up on one leg, now the other. Stand. "Good boy," I say aloud as I sway about in semidelirium, hoping that I will cool off and my head will clear. The wind flash-dries the drops of seawater trickling down my body, escorting tiny streams of heat away. Sometimes the ritual works. I steady up and remain erect for several minutes. Other times my head feels as if it is being crushed by a heavy weight, my vision fills with swirling bluish haze, and I collapse, using the residue of my senses to guide my fall back into the raft. Yes, I am in much better shape than I thought I'd be by this time, but at high noon I am often "beyond the point of coherent action," as Robertson so dryly puts it. If I can just keep myself together, I can make it to the islands. But how much longer can I hang on like this?

Refiguring my position time and again, I put myself about a thousand miles away. Average speed, twenty-five miles a day. Total passage time, seventy days. If only I can guide myself to Guadeloupe. I've got the raft positioned with the canopy across the wind, and the line astern is just off center to guide *Rubber Ducky III* a little bit south of west just as fast as she can waddle.

From the Canaries I wrote to my parents and friends, "Expect me in Antigua around February 24." That was seven days ago. Yet I also warned them that the trade winds hadn't filled in yet, so I might arrive as late as March 10, seven days hence. If a search is made then, I will still be out of range, way too far out to sea. If only a ship will pick me up soon, those at home won't begin to worry.

I see a shark fin zigzagging in quick pumps across *Ducky's* bow, about a hundred feet away. It's a small fin, but I'm still ·glad that he shows no interest in us. Instead, he slides off to the east against the wind and current to await food that is drifting or swimming with the North Equatorial stream.

Like most predators, sharks cannot afford to be seriously hurt, because an injury or weakness can prevent them from hunting and may even invite an attack from their own kind. So most sharks bump their prey before attacking. If the prey puts up no defense, the shark will dig right in. They will eat anything; license plates and anchors have been found in their stomachs. I wonder about life rafts. I count on their bumping to give me a chance to drive them away. But I also think about *Jaws*. I have heard stories of two great white sharks caught since that film came out. Both of the real sharks were about the same size as the mechanical prop, twenty-five feet long, and weighed upward of four tons. Great whites are an unpredictable species. They are so big, ferocious, and powerful that they know no natural enemies and never worry about their prey putting up a significant defense. They give no warning of their attacks and have been known to smash boats and even attack whales.

Then there are orcas, or killer whales, known to have blown large yachts apart. I look at my little aluminum and plastic spear, weighing maybe a pound or two. The point might cause a small shark as much pain as I would feel from a mosquito bite. Even if a small shark forces a showdown at high noon, I'll be pathetically slow to the draw. I'd love the option to get out of this town.

With shivering nights and scorching days, only dusk and dawn offer a little comfort. As the sun drops to the horizon, things begin to cool off. I lounge back again as I did in the morning, flip the sleeping bag over my legs, pump up *Ducky*'s sagging limbs, and watch the sky's grand finale through my picture window. The sharp white disk peeks out now and again from behind the puffy cumulus collected at the horizon. It is past noon in Antigua. If only I had a raft that could sail at a moderate three knots, I'd be snug in harbor already. I'll make it anyway . . . if only I can summon strength I never knew I had.

As the clouds mill about and wander into the sunset, I prepare my dinner, choosing various pieces of fish for a balanced meal: a few chewy sticks, which I regard as sausages, an especially prized fatty belly steak, and a piece of backbone bacon with thin strips of brown, crunchy flesh. I crack the backbone apart and drop gelatinous nuggets of fluid from between the vertebrae onto my board. A noodle runs down the spine, and I add it to the gelatin, making a chicken soup. An invisible Jewish mama coaxes me. "Eat, eat. Go ahead, my sick darling, you must eat your chicken soup to get well." Sumptuous tenderloin steaks come from the meaty back above the organ cavity. I choose a couple of fully dried sticks for toast, since they are overcooked and crunchy. The real treats are the organs, when I have them. Biting into the stomach and intestines is like chewing on a Uniroyal tire, so I don't bother with them, but all else I consume with delight, especially the liver, roe, heart, and eyes. The eyes are amazing, spherical fluid capsules an inch in diameter. Their thin, tough coverings are quite like polystyrene Ping-Pong balls. My teeth crush out a large squirt of fluid, a chewy dewdrop lens, and a papery thin, green-skinned cornea.

I spend an increasing amount of time thinking about food. Fantasies about an inn-restaurant become very detailed. I know how the chairs will be arranged and what the menu will offer. Steaming sherried crab overflows flaky pie shells bedded on rice pilaf and toasted almonds. Fresh muffins puff out of pans. Melted butter drools down the sides of warm, broken bread. The aroma of baking pies and brownies wafts through the air. Chilly mounds of ice cream stand firm in my mind's eye. I try to make the visions melt away, but hunger keeps me awake for hours at night. I am angry with the pain of hunger, but even as I eat it will not stop.

I save the bulk of my water ration for dessert. Since I have rebuilt my stock, I can afford to drink a half pint during the day and three-quarters of a pint at dinner, and still have a couple of ounces for the night. I slowly roll a mouthful around on my tongue until the water is absorbed rather than swallowed. When I return, ice cream will be no more pleasurable.

In these moments of peace, deprivation seems a strange sort of gift. I find food in a couple hours of fishing each day, and I seek shelter in a rubber tent. How unnecessarily complicated my past life seems. For the first time, I clearly see a vast difference between human needs and human wants. Before this voyage, I always had what I needed—food, shelter, clothing, and companionship—yet I was often dissatisfied when I didn't get everything I wanted, when people didn't meet my expectations, when a goal was thwarted, or when I couldn't acquire some material goody. My plight has given me a strange kind of wealth, the most important kind. I value each moment that is not spent in pain, desperation, hunger, thirst, or loneliness. Even here, there is richness all around me. As I look out of the raft, I see God's face in the smooth waves, His grace in the dorado's swim, feel His breath against my cheek as it sweeps down from the sky. I see that all of creation is made in His image. Yet despite His constant company, I need more. I need more than food and drink. I need to feel the company of other human spirits. I need to find more than a moment of tranquility, faith, and love. A ship. Yes, I still need a ship.

The sea has flattened. All is still. Inside of me I feel a symphony of excitement growing, like music that begins very low, almost inaudible, then grows stronger and stronger until the entire audience is swept up in it with a single synchronized, thumping heartbeat. I rise to scan the horizon. Blowing up from astern are gigantic clumps of cumulonimbus clouds. Rain bursts from their flat, black bottoms, above which thick, snowy fleece billows up to great heights, until it is blown off in anvil heads of feathery ice crystals. The clouds push bright blue sky ahead of their walls of gray rain streaking to earth. An invisible paintbrush suddenly splashes a full rainbow of sharply defined color from one horizon to the other. The top of its arc comes directly overhead, lost in turbulent white ten thousand feet up. The breeze caresses my face; the canopy of the raft snaps. The smooth, slate sea is broken with white tumbling cracks. The sun suddenly pops out between billowing sky sculptures far to the west and balances on the horizon. It sends warmth tracking to the east upon its path, heats my back, and sets the bright orange canopy aglow. Another invisible brush stroke paints another perfect rainbow inside and behind the first. Between their belts of color are walls of deep gray. The smaller rainbow is a cavernous mouth well lit on the rim, leading inward to a deeper, electric blue. I feel as if I am passing down the corridor of a heavenly vault of irreproducible grandeur and color. The dorados leap in very high arcs as if they are trying to reach the clouds, catching the setting sun on their sparkling skins. I stand comfortably, back to the sun, as cool rain splashes on my face, fills my cup, and washes me clean. Far away to the north and south the ends of the rainbows touch the sea. Four rainbow ends and no pots of gold, but the treasure is mine nonetheless. Perhaps until now I have always looked for the wrong kind of coin.

As the spectacle moves on, I empty the captured water into containers, pull the sleeping bag over me and close my eyes. My body is sore, but I am strangely at peace. For a short while I feel as if I've moved off of that seat in hell. The benign routine lasts three days. Sometimes for better, sometimes for worse, nothing lasts forever.

By the night of March 6, it is blowing like hell again. All night I am thrown about; it's like trying to sleep in a bumper car. The next day the gale reachs forty knots.

MARCH 6
DAY 30

Combers crash down on *Rubber Ducky,* and I wonder if the strong wind will pick us up and fly us to Antigua. Keeping watch is out of the question. The entrance is lashed down tight. Even tending the still is impossible. If only I had windows, I could see what's going on outside before it leaps inside, and maybe I would see a ship that could get me out of this mess.

Patiently waiting for the gale to blow over, I chew on a fish stick. Dorado skin is much too tough to bite through, so I rake the meat off with my teeth. I feel a hard, sharp object in my mouth, like a shard of bone. I fish it out and find that it is plastic. Part of the cap that covers one of my front teeth has been chipped off. When I was young, the cap came off a few times, and I have vivid memories of the stabbing pain that ran down the exposed nerve of the uncapped tooth stub and shot into my brain. I can feel that some of the cap remains over the nerve, but it is loose and can't last much longer.

Water dribbles in constantly through the canopy. On March 8, *Ducky* is knocked down again. I bail out the gallons of water and begin to wring out the heavy lump that is supposed to be a sleeping bag. My cap is completely gone, but amazingly the tooth doesn't hurt at all. The nerve must have died. Thank heaven for small miracles. I haven't slept for two days. My skin is white, and even my wrinkles have wrinkles. My hair sits dripping and tangled on my head. Fish scales cling to me like ornamental slivers of nail polish. With a gap in the middle of my smile, I must be quite a mess, a real hag. Well, we rafties can't be at our charming best all of the time.

Two hours later *Ducky* is knocked down again. I sit among the floating debris, exhausted, giving in, no longer able to keep cool. Beating my fists in a splashing tantrum, I yell, "You god-damned son-of-a-bitch ocean!" For five minutes I do nothing but curse the wind and sea. I break down sobbing: "Why me? Why does it have to be me? I just want to go home, that's all. Why can't I just go home?" Inside, a second voice scolds me to stop acting like a child. But I'm beyond control. I yell back at myself. "I don't give one damn about being reasonable! I'm hurt, hungry, tired, and scared. I want to cry." So I do.

What I do not know is that this same day, perhaps at this very moment, my father is calling the U.S. Coast Guard to notify them that *Napoleon Solo* is overdue. Sometime before, my mother had had a nightmare. She had seen me clawing through black waters, struggling to regain the surface. She awoke with a start, sweating, shaking, and had been tense ever since, awaiting word from me. None came.

After a few minutes, the fire inside me subsides. I set about the endless, heavy work of bailing and wringing things out. Perhaps when I get back I will have a picnic with friends and neighbors. Yes, I must return for that. There will be laughter and children and fresh-cut grass, pine trees and trout ponds. I'll have them at last. We will have a brontosaurus of a barbecue, trees of salads, and hills of ice cream. People will ask me what it was like. I will tell them I hated it, all of it. There was not one slimy corner that did not stink. You can never love it. You can only do what you must. I hated the sea's snapping off shots of heavy rifle fire next to my ear, rolling heavy stones over me, ripping wounds open, beating me, winning. Weeks on end, no bells, no rounds, continued onslaught. I even hated the equipment that saved my life — the primitive raft that was an aimless, drifting pig of a boat, the wretched tent that turned clean water foul. I hated having to catch drinking water in the same box I had to defecate in. I hated having to haul aboard lovely creatures and tear into their flesh like a beast. I hated counting minutes for thirty-two days. I hated . . . I hated . . .

I did not know a man could have so much hatred and so much longing within him. Yes, I will get home somehow. I must. Has the wind eased a little or is it my imagination?

No. For the next two days the gale continues and life is hellish. I have managed to catch another triggerfish, my third, and another dorado, my fourth. The dorado bent the spear again. I must ration the use of my equipment. Who knows how many dorados it will take to break my spear beyond repair? And how long must the spear last?

MARCH 10
DAY 34

The distillate collection bag of the solar still was nearly full an hour ago. Now it hangs flaccid. A tiny, burred hole has been bitten from one edge of the bag. Friggin' triggerfish. I've lost over six ounces of water. That's a half day of life gone, old boy.

Won't you feel like a jerk if you die just one half day before being picked up?

By March 11 things have calmed again, and I resume my more placid routine. I'm about halfway to the West Indies. Once again I have time to count my blessings. *Solo* stayed afloat long enough for me to salvage what I needed. My equipment is all working, and doing a fair job of it, too. Mountain climbing, camping, Boy Scouts, boat building, sailing, and design, and my family's continued encouragement to confront life head on have all given me enough skill to "seastead" on this tiny, floating island. I am getting there. So far it is a tale of miracles.

On March 13, however, I'm not feeling too chipper. Because of the bad weather, the last dorado that I caught never dried properly and turned pasty and ran-   MARCH 13 cid. I haven't eaten much, and I finally throw   DAY 37 it out. I strain to do my yoga exercises, accomplishing in an hour and a half what usually takes only a half hour. Even in the calm of evening, I don't think I can last much longer.

Doing just enough to hang on will no longer do. I must keep myself in the best shape possible. I must eat more. I pull in the string farm trailing astern and rake off the barnacles with the blade of my knife. I scrape some rust from the peanut and coffee cans into my drinking water in the hope of absorbing some iron and alleviating anemia.

I talk to the lazy vagrant in control of my body. I coax him to kneel by the entrance to await another dorado. At first my body is slow. A dorado swims out. I clumsily splash down. Miss. Another. Miss. But the pumping of blood helps to revive my other self, the physical part. On the third shot I ram my weapon through the fish's back. It pulls me down over the tube as it twists and jerks to get away. I play the fish as if he's on a light line, because I don't want to break or bend my lance. However, I must also retrieve it as quickly as possible, before it can escape. So I let it twist and jerk while I reach down and grab the shaft close to the body; then I lift it up without the risk of bending the shaft. I flip the fish inside, onto the sailcloth blanket that protects the floor. When I get the dorado pinned down with my knees, I slip the cutting board under its head just behind the gills, push my knife into the lateral line, and break the spine with a quick twist of the blade. Usually I completely clean the fish before eating, but now I'm very hungry. I simply gut it and place the rest aside.

By midafternoon I am eating the organs, and I feel as if I have had a transfusion. The dorado's stomach seems full of something. I cut it open. Five partially digested flying fish spill out onto the floor. I hesitate, take a small taste of a flyer, and almost vomit. I gather them up and toss them out. As soon as they are in the air I think, Fool! You should have washed them off and then tried them. Next time. But such a waste of five fish. I mop up the spilled stomach juices and finish cleaning the dorado. Sweat pours off of my head as I squat over my catch and labor in the heat to slice up the body. I stop twice to stretch out my legs and to relieve my cramped knees and back. The work is hard, but I move fast so that I can rest sooner. I always work that way—pushing myself as hard as I can so I can finish quickly and then find complete rest.

As I poke holes through the fish sticks in order to string them up, SLAM! *Rubber Ducky* crushes me between her tubes. Water dribbles in and she springs back to her normal shape as though nothing has happened. It takes me a moment to get my wind back and recover from the shock. The average wave height is only about three feet, but a monster leisurely rolls off ahead. I set to work again with a shrug. I am getting used to various levels of disaster striking with no warning.

The still lies lifeless, draped flat over the bow. It must have gotten smacked pretty hard. Air jets out of it almost as quickly as I can blow it in. The cloth across the bottom, which allows excess seawater to drain through and which is airtight when wet, now sports a hole. The cloth has deteriorated from the constant cycles of wetting and drying and from chafing against *Ducky*'s tubes. Less than thirty days of use, and the still is gonzo. I've never been able to coerce my remaining still to work. As we have drifted west, the number of light showers has increased, but I am lucky when I can trap six or eight ounces of water within a week. Another critical safety margin has disappeared. I'm in big trouble—not that I've been out of big trouble for quite a while now.

I must get the other still to work and keep it working, perhaps for longer than thirty days. I blow it up until it's tight as a tick. Just below the skirt through which the lanyard passes, a tiny mouth whistles a single-note tune until the balloon's lungs are emptied. The hole is in a tight corner and on a lumpy seam, which makes it impossible to effectively wedge a piece of repair tape into it. Making something watertight is difficult enough, even for a boat builder in an equipped shop. To make something airtight is an even taller order.

For hours I try to think of a way to seal the leaking still. Perhaps I can burn some pieces of plastic from the old still or its packaging and drip the melted globs over the hole. But I find that my matches are sodden and my lighter has been drained of fluid. So I wedge the tape in as firmly as I can and grouchily reinflate the still every half hour. Each time, the still begins to slump as soon as I stop pumping. Water begins to collect in the distillate bag, but it is salty. At this pace, I already feel like I have a case of lockjaw, and my mouth is very dry. I must find an effective solution. If only I had some silicone seal or other kind of good goop.

MARCH 16
DAY 40

I have managed to last forty days, but my water stock is declining, and I have but a few hard pieces of fish dangling in the butcher shop. It is also a little disconcerting to realize that *Ducky* is guaranteed for forty days of use. If she fails me now, do you suppose I *can* get my money back?

Despite these problems, I have good reason to celebrate this milestone. I've lasted longer than I had dreamed possible in the beginning. I'm over halfway to the Caribbean. Each day, each hardship, each moment of suffering, has brought me another small step closer to salvation. The probability of rescue, as well as gear failure, continually increases. I imagine two stone-faced poker players throwing chips onto a pile. One player is named Rescue and the other is Death. The stakes keep getting bigger and bigger. The pile of chips now stands as tall as a man and as big around as a raft. Somebody is going to win soon.

The dorados begin their morning foray. They bang away at the bottom of the raft and sometimes run around the outside, cracking stiff shots against the raft with their tails. I grab my spear and wait. Sometimes I have a little trouble focusing. During the last gale I jabbed my eye with a piece of the polypropylene line I've rigged to keep the still in place. After a couple of days of oozing and swelling, my eye cleared up, but I was left with a spot in my vision, which I often take to be a glimpse of an airplane or the first hint of a fish shooting out before the tip of my spear. Dorados are so fast that my shot must be instantaneous, without thought, like a bolt of lightning. A head, a microsecond of hesitation, a splash, a strike, a hard pull on my arm, and an escape. On other days I've hit two or three morning and evening but most of the time come up with nothing. This morning I'm lucky and catch a nice fat female. Squatting over her for two hours on the rolling floor of the raft is hard work for my matchstick legs. Finally the job is done and the fish hung up to dry. I begin to mop up the blood and scales, but my sponges have turned to useless little globs. Evidently the stomach juices that I swabbed up from the last dorado have digested them. Since my sleeping bag has proven its ability to soak up water, I take out some of the batting and bind this up with pieces of codline to use as sponges.

Each day now I set my priorities, based on my continuing analysis of raft condition, body condition, food, and water. Each day at least one factor lags behind what I consider adequate.

The dismal problem of collecting or distilling water is one I must find a solution to.

I take some of the black cloth wick from the first still, the one that I cut up early in the game. I affix it across the hole of the still with the rotted bottom, letting the still's weight keep it in place. I now have one still aft and one forward, in the only positions available for frequent tending. Every ten minutes throughout the day, I am a human bellows at the service of one or the other still. In between inflations, I empty the distillate just in case salt water sneaks in to pollute it while I'm not watching. By nightfall I have collected a full two pints of fresh water. I am continually paying higher prices for my small successes. The work is demanding and boils off a lot of body fluid. I can't decide if my steaming cells gain anything from the exercise. There is little time to dream these days, barely enough time to live, but fruit mountains still stand in the panorama of my mind's eye.

The next day my debate over the value of operating both stills becomes moot. The entire cloth bottom on the older still gives way. Throughout the day I keep the one still working and try to devise a patch for the old. I painstakingly poke holes around the rim of the opening, using my awl, then thread through sail twine and sew on a new cloth bottom. I try to seal it with the bits of tape that I have left, but the patch remains an utter failure. The still lies dead no matter how hard and fast I try to resuscitate it.

Luckily I'm learning about the personality of the new still. The inside black cloth wick is wetted by seawater dripping through a valve on the top of the still. The rate at which the inside wick is wetted is critical to production of fresh water. If it's too wet, it doesn't heat up efficiently. Instead, the excess, warm seawater just passes out through the bottom cloth. If the wick is too dry, there is less than the maximum amount of water available for evaporation. I must maximize the rates at which the water will evaporate, collect on the inside of the plastic balloon, condense, and finally drop into the distillate collection bag. It seems that the inside pressure of the still affects the rate of dripping through the valve. The still seems most efficient at a pressure that allows it to sag, but not so much that the wick hits the plastic balloon, because if that happens the salt water in the wick is drawn into the distillate. To keep her at just the right inflation requires constant attention.

To help prevent another failure of the bottom cloth, I make a diaper for the still out of a square of sailcloth and add padding, using the cloth wicking from the cut-up still. I blanket the bottom of the still by tying the diaper up by its corners to the lanyard skirt, hoping the diaper will take the chafe from *Ducky* and will keep the bottom cloth constantly wet to delay rotting.

My rain collection systems also need improvement. At the first *thrrrap* of water droplets from the sky, I usually wedge the Tupperware box against the aft side of the still. It's held in place by the still bridle. The arrangement is simple and is quick to rig or empty, which is important in order to minimize salt water pollution from breaking waves and spray. However, I think that I can catch more water if I can find a way to mount the Tupperware box on top of the raft. I need to put a bridle around the box so that I have something to secure it with. The awl on my jackknife has a cutting edge, so I wind it into the plastic lip that runs around the box, boring a hole in each corner. Through these I string a collar made of sail twine. I secure the two ends of one bridle to *Ducky*'s tail, lead the middle of it to the top of the arch tube, and equip it with a quick-release metal clip that I've stolen from one of the stills. Forward, I tie a short lanyard to the canopy entrance and affix a second clip to the other end, which I also lead to the peak of the canopy. When I have to use the Tupperware for some other purpose, I leave the two clips hooked together, so that they are always ready. As soon as it begins to rain, I can quickly flip the clips onto the collar of the box, which keeps it pretty secure on the apex of the arch tube, angled more directly into the wind and higher

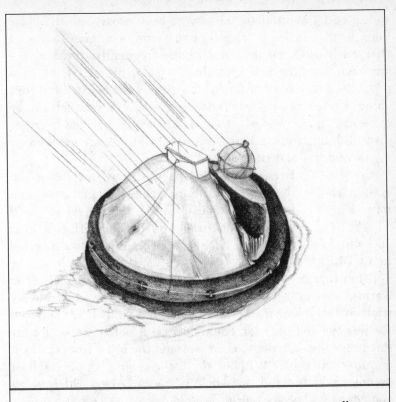

The Tupperware box is twice as effective as a rain collector when I rig it up on top of the raft. The bridle that secures it to *Ducky*'s stern can be quickly released. It is clipped to the box's string collar. A matching clip and bridle faces forward, out of view. The box may then be used for other purposes between rainfalls by removing it and clipping the two hooks together.

away from the waves. Its biggest benefit is that it is no longer blanketed from rainfall by the canopy, which is now below it. In fact, it will prove twice as effective this way.

Finally I must tend to my steel knives. My Cub Scout jack-knife with the awl is one that I found when I was twelve. The spring on its main blade has always been broken, so the blade flops about a little. It's a ball of rust now. I scrape it clean. I sharpen both it and my sheath knife frequently. Rubbing the steel hard against fish skin that has a tissue of fat attached produces a tiny drool of fat, which greases the blades until they shine. I treasure raw materials and basic tools; so much can be done with them. Paper, rope, and knives have always been my favorite human inventions. And now, all three are essential to my own sanity and survival.

MARCH 18
DAY 42

Each day seems longer. On my forty-second in the raft, the sea is as flat and hot as an equatorial tin roof in August. The sun in the sky is joined by hundreds that flash from water ripples. It is all I can do to try to move about in *Ducky*. We sit like a period in a book of blank pages.

I find that my sleeping bag helps to keep me cool as well as warm. I spread it out over the floor to dry in the sun. When I stick my legs under it, they are shaded and sandwiched between the wet bag and the cool, damp floor. It is not very good for my sores, but they are not too bad now and the relief from the heat is quite noticeable. Without the bag covering, the black floor becomes very hot and the whole inside of *Ducky*, which is hot enough as is, becomes an unbearable oven.

Nothing to do but wait for the wind and try to score more food. Some good fresh guts should help lift my spirits. Triggers, a school of them, flap up toward the side of the raft, then disappear under it, come up again, pirouette, dive, loop, and roll about each other in an amazing underwater ballet. They are very wary of me now and are becoming more difficult to catch than the dorados. They don't have the same sustained speed, but in quick little jerks they can dodge my spear deftly. They flirt just outside of my reach. Jab. Miss. I must two-arm a hit on a dorado, but maybe I can get a quick and penetrating one-arm shot on a trigger. Jab. Jab. Their waving fins taunt me. My arm snaps out straight; a trigger takes the spear in his belly. Inside the fish, I find large white sacs—must be the male organs—that I will soon treasure as much as the female's golden eggs.

Ducky, can't you please stop flopping about? You're bound to be sending out a general invitation to every shark in the district. Maybe I should get more fish while things are so flat.

The sun sinks down to the horizon once again, and the dorados collect for evening recess. They seem mesmerized by the calm conditions and glide about like phantoms, gently nudging us. The emerald elders still skirt the vicinity, keeping an eye on their school. I am coming to know individuals not only by their size, markings, and scars but also by their personalities. I am getting very attached to them. Some like to strike one side of the raft, while others prefer another. Some strike aggressively and quickly fly away, as if they are angry or are testing my strength. Others softly slide along the bottom and wiggle out . . . right . . . in . . . front. Fire! I hit too far aft, near the tail. She churns the surface and shakes loose. I rest.

Clouds sit like dirty fingerprints across a silver sun that reaches down to touch the horizon. Bands of light, "Jesus rays," strike out across the heavens. On the eastern horizon, the sky has reached a deep blue, soon to be black and filled with twinkling stars. The soft, round waves remind me of long stretches of ripe wheat fields. Bending to a gentle breeze that marks where invisible heavens touch the earth, the heavy-headed stalks bow their heads and await the reaper's scythe. I haven't much time to fish. I take up my pose again.

A big form appears to my left. By now I'm used to awaiting the perfect shot, but I may not get another this evening. What the hell. Without thinking, without fear of battle with another male, I roll to the right and jab the spear to the left. Humph! Solid hit. All is still.

Where is the fury? I'm grasping the gun tightly, leaning over the tubes, frozen. In a second the battle will begin. But it doesn't. In his huge head the eye is glazed. His slightly opened mouth is paralyzed. His gills are glued shut. The tip of the spear rests in the stripe that runs down his side, which marks the position of his spine. The barb is still barely visible. The spear has not been driven straight through. I gently pull him toward me, grab the spear with my other hand, and ever so carefully begin to lift. It's like juggling a ball on the end of a stick. What a relief not to endure another dangerous battle. He is food for a week. The glassy surface bubbles up as his body begins to rise. Taking the weight now . . . Splash. I lunge to grab him. Too late. His smooth skin slips from my fumbling fingers.

The big, stiff body whirls downward like a bright dead leaf falling from a limb. His blank stare goes round and round as he sinks deeper and deeper. All of the other dorados have been watching. Like fingers reaching down to him, they descend. Deeper, still deeper. Finally their shapes converge like living petals blooming from the stamen of the dead fish. The tiny flower whirls ever deeper, getting smaller and smaller, until it is no more. The sun is gone. The waters become black and empty. I stare into the depths.

CRIES AND WHISPERS

ON MARCH 9

the New York Coast Guard instructed stations in Virginia and Puerto Rico to broadcast a standard yacht-overdue message on their offshore "Notices to Mariners," which is usually monitored by commercial and pleasure craft venturing in deep waters. Through Lloyds of London, the Guard traced me to the Canaries. Since there was no official record that I was ever on Hierro, they refused to believe that I left the island at the end of January. Only when my mother and father give them a copy of my letter postmarked on Hierro do they believe my parents are correct. This kind of mistrust of emotionally involved amateurs in the search-and-rescue (SAR) business will characterize their handling of my case and will lead to some bureaucratic embarrassment. The Coast Guard next conducts a harbor check in the West Indies to see if *Napoleon Solo* has arrived without notification.

No one knows exactly when I left the Canaries or whether I took a direct route, swung south to catch the trades, or sailed via the Cape Verde Islands. My family knows I did not take the Cape Verde route, but the Guard cannot be certain. The ocean is an unbelievably vast wilderness. Pinpointing a vessel, even when its approximate position is known, is literally more difficult than finding a needle in a haystack. Even if my position could be approximated within a hundred miles, a circular area two hundred miles across, covering over thirty thousand square miles, would have to be searched in order to locate me. What the Coast Guard does not tell my family is that if I am more than a week overdue, I am most likely dead. It happens all the time. Three hundred seventy-four sailors died in U.S. waters between 1972 and 1977 in commercial fishing accidents alone. Coast Guard funding has been cut, so they are understaffed and under-equipped. Besides, even if they send out a search party they won't find me. I am still so far out to sea that I am out of range of an effective search. The Guard tells my family that sending aircraft to look for *Napoleon Solo* is out of the question.

Meanwhile, back in my raft, though I still scan the sky for any sign of a plane, I am painfully aware of the improbability of seeing one.

By March 18, my forty-second day in the raft, the Coast Guard has finished the harbor check, which has concentrated on the French and English West Indies. No one has seen *Solo*.

Each night I sleep for about an hour and a half at a time before a clump of hair is pulled out by *Ducky*'s rubber or cramps in my legs deepen to the point that I must move. I get up, look around, and lie down again in one of the other two semicomfortable positions. The moon has been bitten away to nothing, grown round and fat again, and is now being devoured a second time through the endless progression of nights. Despite my worries, especially about sudden terminal damage to my raft by sharks or other creatures, all is holding together and I feel well rested. I arise on March 19 as usual, hoping that this day will hold the key to my release.

I cannot stop mourning the big dorado that I futilely slew last evening. I try to convince myself that my depression comes only from the fact that I am in desperate need of meat, but my sense of loss is not solely pragmatic. Ineffectual attempts to catch fish are nothing new, and I think little of them. I feel emotionally devastated. The dorados have become much more than food to me. They are even more than pets. I look upon them as equals—in many ways as my superiors. Their flesh keeps me alive. Their spirits keep me company. Their attacks and their resistance to the hunt make them worthy opponents, as well as friends. I am thankful for their meat and companionship and fearful of their power. I wonder if my deep respect for them is related to my Indian ancestors' respect for all natural forces. It is strange how killing animals can sometimes inspire such worship of them. I can justify killing the dorados in order

MARCH 19
DAY 43

to save my own life, but even that is getting more difficult. Last night's killing was to no one's advantage. I have robbed the fish of life and myself of the fish's spirit. I feel as if I have gravely sinned, that this is a very bad omen. Such waste. How I hate waste. Still, I realize that if I am to survive I must continue to fish. I must prepare myself to kill again this morning.

A large plastic loop is riveted onto the tip of the aluminum tubing of my spear gun. The arrow used to shoot through the loop but now lies tightly bound through it. I detect a crack in the plastic. The fitting is near the end of its life. If the fitting breaks, the slender silver arrow might be twisted off and pulled out. If I lose it, I'll have nothing with which to fish. I add some lashings to further secure the arrow shaft to the plastic tip and the plastic tip to the aluminum tubing. It looks ridiculously secure, but I know that the whole rig is tenuous at best. I wonder how many more dorados it will last.

The fish begin their gala morning procession. A head appears directly under my point. I thrust down and drive clear through the body, which immediately becomes a somersaulting monster, practically whipping the gun from my grip. I hold. No! The plastic gun tip explodes, lashings fly apart and tangle in the air, the arrow's metal butt is snapped cleanly off, and the arrow is torn off the gun shaft. I dive forward, trying to grab the spear, but it flips forward with a splash. A horrendous sound like the ripping open of a huge stiff zipper meets my ears. The dorado has run the sharp tip into the bottom tube of the raft. Air blows out in a spluttering, heinous burble.

The fish is free. Somehow I've managed to keep the gun and spear in my hands. I cast them inside and grab hold of the tear. Oh my God! It's a gaping hole, a mouth about four inches long. I try to roll the lips together, but *Ducky* continues to sink. Huge bubbles explode from the opening, then smaller bubbles, rolling out more slowly. Finally, the bottom tube lies flat and still.

It is over. *Rubber Ducky* has settled so that she is supported by her top tube. There are now about three inches of freeboard. Waves slosh in over the top. Water pressure under the raft pushes the floor upward. The pressure yanks the bottom tube from my grasp and pulls it under, giving the floor enough extra material to bulge up to sea level. I struggle to move through the rubber quicksand, trying to locate my equipment, which has been swallowed up.

If I cannot repair the damage, I will not last long. It will be impossible to stay dry, and salt water sores will bore into my skin. My legs stick into the sea. Now passing sharks will grab these rather than the ballast pockets. The fish already batter and bite my limbs through the rubber. I won't be able to sleep. My legs hang down so deeply that when the dorados bump they will be well below the range of my spear. Even if I do catch fish, I won't be able to dry it, and it will soon turn to inedible muck. *Ducky* is wobbling more than ever, and that will increase chafing on the still. I must do something and do it quickly while the weather holds.

The conical plugs from the repair kit are much too small to stop up the tear. Perhaps a piece of foam from the small cushion that I got out of *Solo* will work. Fortunately it is closed-cell foam made of billions of tiny bubbles, rather than open-cell, which is made of similar bubbles but with burst walls. Closed-cell foam doesn't absorb water and is airtight as well. Ignoring the dorado's beatings, I find my tools and set to work as fast as I can. I cut a strip of foam and several pieces of light line, lean over the bow, and pull at the bottom tube against the weight of my equipment and myself. The tear is close enough to open it up, but still out of sight. I stuff the foam plug in, grab the top and bottom lip, lasso them with the line, and tightly wind the line around. The line hasn't caught the outside edges of the mouth, so I add more line, trying to work it inboard of the first line. The windings pull the mouth into enough of a pucker to enclose its edges. The patch pokes out like flounder lips with a little foam tongue hanging out. Time to try it out. The pump whimpers. The tube begins to bloat, pulling the floor a little tighter. As *Ducky* begins to rise, the underwater gurgling breaks the surface, and the mouth rears up and hisses at me like a sea serpent. Within fifteen minutes the tube is soft again, and my body sinks into the rubber quicksand.

I lean back over the side. Air is escaping from the numerous wrinkles in the material, which spread from the puckered tear like roots from a tree trunk. I test batting from the sleeping bag to use as a caulking, but even when densely compressed, air flows through it. My old gloppy sponges may be effective if I cover them with collars of foam strips. For five hours I try to fill the gaps in the seal. Each time I pump up the tube, a trickle of bubbles breaks the surface. I push in more caulking, but the bubbles multiply and grow larger. To keep the tube tolerably inflated requires fifty pumps every half hour. Three thousand pumps will be needed each day to keep *Rubber Ducky III* alive. That's over two hours of grueling exercise, about twice what I think my body can manage. When the seas rebuild, if the patch holds at all, I'll probably have to double my efforts. It's impossible.

We're about six hundred miles out to sea, thirty-four days from landfall at best. The deflated bottom tube is acting like a sea anchor, slowing *Ducky*'s drift. Working hard in the intense heat, my mouth salty from holding line and knife between my teeth, I have reached a new, desperate level of thirst. My muscles are already spent. I'll never last thirty-four days.

Lying back, I feel the tube deflate once again. I try to rest and stay calm. Perhaps there is a shipping lane between Brazil and the southern coast of the United States, about three hundred miles away. Still too far. I feel as if I've been taken off my seat in hell only to be thrown into the fire.

My mind wanders to the many repair devices that might be effective—needles, sail twine, and good goop; a huge hemostat type of scissors-vise; maybe a balloon that could be inserted and blown up—but such materials are to be found only 120 leagues to the west. The only solution I can think of is to push a plug into the hole and lash it up tight. How I miss the inspirational advice and hope, the ingenuity, creativity, and charity, of a helping hand.

A bank of clouds slides by to the north. I must beat the weather. A sliver of moon sits in a very black sky like a dreamy eye opened just enough to watch the sleeping sea. I tie my flashlight tightly to the top of my head, like a makeshift miner's helmet. All of the equipment is secured to the windward side to keep it from tumbling down on me. Precut light-line laces hang from the fish strings within easy, one-arm reach. With my nose to the water, I can just see the damaged area. I don't much like reaching down into the blackness. Slowly I work loose and remove the rat's nest of lines and plug. The beam of light shines down upon the still water and catches small fish yards below. From how deep can the beacon be seen? Will it attract fish? I begin to reinsert the plug. The beam is suddenly eclipsed by a huge gray shape sliding by just inches from my hands. I jerk them from the water. The shark is about ten feet long. Average. He lazily swings around the raft, breaks the surface for a moment, and then resubmerges. I thrust at him several times with the spear, but it is like trying to move a mountain with a toothpick. He lazily mops his tail this way and that as if he doesn't even feel the point. I do not see him for some time. Now the awakened eye of the moon is higher and brighter. I bend to work again, forcing the plug deep into the tear, carefully cinching it with the line, winding, pulling hard, winding. SHARP TEETH! My hands catapult from the water. Adrenalin must be oozing from my quaking skin. I flip the flashlight back on. A triggerfish whirls about the patch and disappears. My watch! Of course—the glowing hands and numerals. The trigger must have thought it was edible. I take it off and again dip into the ocean.

The bottom tube has to be completely deflated. Then I can pull a sufficient amount of material up around the plug and lash it into a big enough pucker that the line can catch the outside corners of the mouth. An effective plug will shorten the outside circumference of the raft by four or more inches. When the cheeks behind the mouth inflate, they will try to stretch it back out to its original shape and stretch the mouth out flat. Two and one-half pounds per square inch is the pressure that must be resisted. Using my forearm as a lever and the top tube as a fulcrum, I pull the lashings so tight the lines cut my hands and the top tube rubs so harshly against my forearm lever that it chafes a large hole through the skin.

It's still no good. The patch leaks almost as fast as I can pump it up. I'm so exhausted that I fall asleep, rolling around in my soggy ship.

I awake at dawn, ready for another try. As I expected, when the bottom tube is inflated, the lips are pulled out flat enough for a corner to slip out from under the lashings. Bubbles snigger out from this side. I stuff shards of foam and balls of gooey sponge into the crevice and tie it to the main plug. A gray hulk with white-tipped fins slips under me. The damned water buzzard is still here, lolling about, biding his time, circling, waiting.

MARCH 20
DAY 44

I have retied my spear together, being very careful to make it tight enough that I can neither pull the arrow out nor loosen the lashings. It's a pretty stiff rig. I jab at the shark when I can, but he banks and swoops, gliding just out of range. When I do strike, he ignores my puny stings. I continue my work. I fit a collar of foam around the primary and secondary plugs, and pump up. Air bubbles stream out from every wrinkle of the dentureless mouth. Sixty pumps each half hour, or my legs will poke down like sausages, free for the tasting. I'm getting angry. The beast comes in close. I wait for him, hatred screwing up my face. I rise as high as I can and ram the spear down with all my weight, making a dead-center hit on the lateral line that runs down the side of his head and back. This line is so sensitive it can pick up the vibrations of a struggling wounded fish over a quarter mile away. Within a second he has disappeared, shooting through the depths like a *Millennium Falcon* from *Star Wars* jumping to hyperspace.

I tie a line from the boarding-ladder anchor loop across the

The damned water buzzard is still there, lolling about,
biding his time, circling, waiting.

patch up to the handline. By pulling on the line, I can put enough outside pressure on the patch that the leak significantly slows. I add a couple of tourniquets as well. At last, *Ducky* requires only forty pumps every two hours, but I hear the constant hissing of the angry serpent looking for any escape route.

Work is burning up the aching muscle tissue in my arms, but there is no rest for the wicked. I must get the still working again and build up my strength. There's no dried fish left. When the dorados come to visit between hunting forays, I am ready. I double-check my spear lashings and get into position. It is all I can do to strike my pose, not to mention a fish. Clumsy, inaccurate, anxious stabs succeed only in thrashing the water and scaring them off. At last one comes within range. Groaning, I drive the shaft down, strike her in the back, but do not get all the way through. She spirals about the end of the arrow at incredible speed and in a moment, before I can grasp my weapon with both hands, she is gone. I look dumfoundedly at the blunt threaded tip of the spear. In less than two seconds, the fish neatly unscrewed the point and left with it. The dorados have awaited their chance to test me. They have destroyed my ship, disarmed me, and now they mock me. If only I were a sea creature. Fish do not get themselves into problems that they must use intellect and tools to solve. They simply swim, breed, and die. I am awed by the intricate perfection of the world in which I find myself, but I am too tired for true appreciation. Instead, I collapse, depressed. I cannot lift my arms easily, but I must. Now there is more work than ever to do.

I begin to dig through my equipment bag, looking for anything from which to fashion a new point for the spear. In one of the pockets I find a Boy Scout utensil kit made of flat-sheet stainless steel: a knife, fork, and spoon nested together. It's another item that I had kicking around for years and threw into my emergency bag because I had little other need for it. I can try to make a point from either the fork or knife. The fork is sturdiest and may be useful for pronging triggerfish. I decide to try the knife first. Again I use codline for the lashings, winding them as tightly as possible around the knife handle and the arrow shaft. The knife has two holes in it; I tie a string from the aft hole back to the line that retains the arrow and then farther back to the gun handle. Even if the knife is pulled off the end, I won't lose it. The thin blade sticks out several inches forward of the arrow shaft. It feels very wiggly, and I can easily bend it, so I have my doubts about its effectiveness in catching dorados. I'll try it on a trigger first. Even the triggers' tough hide will probably bend the tip over. But they stand off anyway, as if they know I'm rearmed.

Perhaps it's time to try the hook and line again. Gooseneck barnacles make good bait, and they're plentiful enough. I pull up the line that trails astern to the man-overboard pole, scrape off a couple of fat barnacles, slip one on a trout-size hook, and trail it astern. Within the hour I have a fish on the line. Great! Maybe I can live off triggerfish. When I reel in my catch, it suddenly blows up like a balloon, brandishing hundreds of sharp spines. Porcupine fish are notoriously poisonous, and the spines are another threat to poor *Rubber Ducky*. I shake the hook free and try again. The puffer goes at it again. No one else is interested. To hell with it.

Strange wildlife begins to show. Shrill squeaking comes from the water under the raft. Saddleback porpoises appear, keeping their distance. Light and dark streaks mark the stirrups and seats that give them their name. They somersault over one another and move off, leaving behind a touch of their smiling-face spirits. A fish, longer, slimmer, and less colorful than a dorado, whips past. It's too fast and far away to identify clearly.

Clumps of sargasso appear more frequently and take on signs of age, which they lacked further east. They have had time to develop their own ecosystem. Clear eggs sprinkle the branches, many of which are dead, like dewdrops in a graying beard. While I pick out the eggs, a couple of crabs, about one-half inch across and sporting white graphics on their backs, scurry away. One tunnels through the weed, drops out onto the waves, and swims away like a waterbug. The other I grab and pop into my mouth like an M & M. The tiny morsel of crabmeat is a welcome relief from the taste of fish.

Ducky drifts over transparent globes of phytoplankton about an eighth to a quarter inch across. I've seen them on occasion since the beginning of the voyage, but as we drift westward they have collected into thick clumps, and many are always in view. If I had packed nylon stockings into my equipment bag, I could have made plankton nets, which I would trail at night when the large zooplankton orbit to the surface, glowing with phosphorescence. But without an efficient collection system, the tidbits I reap from the weed and waves are far too scant to live on.

I lie back and gaze up into the sky, the only thing I share with those back on dry land. A snowy white bird with two long feathers streaming out from its tail and a Lone Ranger black mask across its eyes flaps wildly about, squawking. I've often watched tropic birds try for hours to perch on top of a pitching mast. I hope that this one is silly enough to land on *Rubber Ducky III*. After a while, the bird flutters on its reckless way in a vague northerly direction.

Each change in wildlife or weed is a sign. Each heralds altering currents and progress west. Am I closer to the continental shelf than I thought? No. That's just wishful thinking, you turkey! My own whimpering accompanies the pumps as I continue the struggle to keep *Ducky* inflated. I'll hang on as long as I can. Then I'll turn on the EPIRB one last time and hope that I'm in range of western flights and that the battery has more juice than I do.

Dougal Robertson's book contains several useful charts. One marks the migration routes of birds, another shows expected rainfall—not much for my area—another the major shipping lanes. My large chart also shows the lanes, as well as currents, winds, and other details. I transfer the outline of the continental shelf from one of Robertson's charts onto my large chart, though the scale of the small charts may be quite inaccurate. None of the charts show any shipping from South to North America, but I reason that there must be a large number of small vessels running an interisland business in the Caribbean, and there should be traffic from Brazil to islands and to other points north. I sketch in my assumed lanes and possible traffic patterns for the airlines, so I will know when to try the EPIRB. I continually calculate the probable error in my navigation, both for and against me, and write on my chart maximum and minimum number of days to the lanes, to the shelf, to the islands. Even the best estimates don't look good, and each day makes the minimum-to-maximum-number-of-days spread wider and wider apart, which gives rise to incredible hope on the one hand, incredible depression on the other. At my current speed of eight miles a day, I'm not getting to any lanes any too quickly.

Before nightfall I take advantage of a sleepy triggerfish, bending my butter-knife point in the process. It takes me almost an hour to clean the little rhino. I waste nothing. Little bits of meat lie around the eyes and along the snout. Fatty fluid can be scraped from the eye sockets. I even cut off the end of the tongue and pretend it's a crunchy water chestnut. Most of the meat is white rawhide, but from between the fins' bones that fan out of the body a little bit of red hamburger can be scraped. I save a few bones in case I need to make an awl.

Night brings a deep sleep, disturbed only by occasional cramps and one shark that rakes *Ducky*'s butt. I drive it off in blasé fashion.

It is March 22, my forty-sixth day. The New York Coast Guard cancels the broadcast that *Napoleon Solo* is overdue. They notify Lloyds of London, Canary Islands authorities, and the Miami and Puerto Rico Coast Guard stations that the "active search has been suspended." They wait until the first of April to notify my family of this.

MARCH 22
DAY 46

I still keep watch as often as I can, scouring the empty horizon for hours each day, exploring every wisp of cloud for the hint of a contrail, straining to hear the faraway rumble of propellers. I know that I'm too far away for a search to be effective and too long overdue for people to believe I'm still alive. Officially I must be "lost without trace." I continue my vigil nonetheless.

Yesterday the leak worsened. I tried to increase outside pressure by securing another retaining line across the patch, but it pulled the plug a little to the side and the serpent's silvery tongue of bubbles lashed out. After several hours of adjustment, I got it caged again, but an evil hiss of air escapes nonstop.

There is often water in the raft these days. My legs push the rubber floor into the sea until I'm about mid-thigh deep, and the water forces the rubber to hug my legs. I feel like I'm wearing flooded hip boots. When I want to move, I have to yank one leg out at a time, struggle to pull it up high enough to clear the bulging bottom, and sink it down again a little closer to my destination, all the while balancing on one leg. When I lose my balance, I fall into the black, clutchy amoeboid, and it's quite a battle to keep from being totally engulfed. It's worse in the middle, of course, so I try to keep to the edges of the raft. Even so, the clinging rubber pulls the heads off of the hundreds of boils that have erupted on my legs and back. Some of the salt water sores are wedged tightly in my crotch and others dot my chest. My body is rotting before my eyes.

I ignore the pain and try to fish. Through my feverish, dizzy vision, I see that I've managed to board two triggers. I have also struck two dorados, but each time the thin knife I'm now using for a spear point simply bent over. Even when I hit dorados hard enough to cut into the flesh, they easily wiggle away. With the blade bending this way and that, I expect it to snap off at any time.

In my bag I find the leather knife with which I cut *Ducky* free from *Solo*'s deck a month and a half ago. I break off the wooden handle, remove the stiff steel blade, and hone it on my

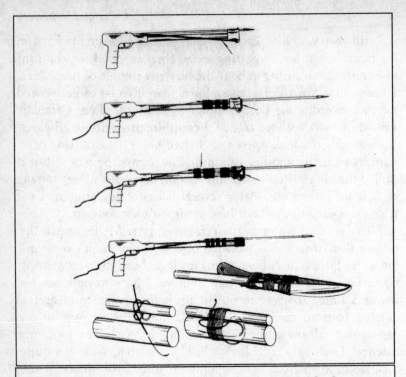

EVOLUTION OF THE SPEAR, *profile views: In the first view,* the arrow indicates the elastic power strap that propelled the spear arrow before it was lost. *In the second view,* I pull the arrow out to maximize the weapon's range, then lash the arrow tightly to the gun shaft. A retaining line from the notch in the butt of the arrow back to the trigger guard assures that the arrow cannot be pulled out forward. The spear arrow still rests through the plastic housing/guide at the tip of the gun. Battles with the dorados put large side loads on the arrow and gun, which is not the normal direction of load for a spear gun. The side loads soon put a crack in the plastic housing, indicated by the drawn arrow. *In the third view,* I attempt to reduce this side movement by pulling the arrow further back onto the gun handle. I also reinforce the plastic tip with additional lashings. However, the next dorado's strength bursts the plastic tip apart, causing the arrow to twist to the side and snap off where indicated by the drawn arrow. Now the fish pulls the arrow out of the aft and middle lashings, leaving only one to hold it onto the gun handle. It twists the arrow around, and rams it into the bottom tube of the raft. In the *bottom profile view,* I lash the arrow directly onto the gun shaft. The retaining line now runs from the foremost lashing back to the trigger guard, so that the lashing cannot be pulled off the end of the gun shaft.

IMPROVING A NEW SPEAR TIP: Finally a dorado unscrews the barbed point of the spear and steals it away. On one side of the shaft I put a stainless steel butter knife. On the other, closer to the viewer, is the blade from a leather knife. Each has holes in the handle ends, so I tie them tightly together, and then wrap them securely with lashings. I bend the handle of the butter knife away from the arrow shaft in order to serve as a barb. Through the hole shown in the handle I attach another retaining line and lead it aft. Even if the knives are pulled off of the end of the arrow shaft, they will still be attached to the raft. To increase penetrating power and to allow the blades to support one another against heavy side loads, I bend the blades so that the tips touch, creating a large V-shaped blade. The foremost lashing extends forward of the arrow shaft so that it helps to keep the blade tips pulled together.

The bottom sketches show the procedure for making a lashing of this type, which is very useful to sailors. *Left:* Tie a clove hitch around one shaft. If you tie it around both, it will twist around them, following your lashing windings, and the lashing will quickly loosen. *Right:* Wind the line around neatly and tightly. Bring the end of the rope up *between* the two shafts, then thread the line through the small gap between the shafts, perpendicular to the windings. These frappings pull the windings very tight and also keep them from wandering. Three or four of these frappings are enough. Finally finish off with another clove hitch, preferably on the shaft and side opposite from which you began. The clove hitch shown is composed of only two turns around the shaft. However, additional turns can create a multiple clove hitch. I usually prefer about four, essentially one clove hitch next to the other. This way, should one turn work loose, the essential hitch, next to the lashing, will remain tight.

stone. I lash the butter knife to one side of the spear shaft and the leather blade to the other, and match up the tips to form a V-shaped arrowhead. Through the holes in their handles, I lash the knives around the spear shaft and to each other. If I have enough strength, the spear will hit the dorado like a meteorite and leave a gaping crater. To increase the point's holding power, I bend the butter-knife handle out from the shaft to act as a barb. These blades are the last pieces of metal I have from which to manufacture a spear point. Losing them may cost me my life. A retaining line from the butter knife to the handle of the gun is my life insurance; I tie the gun to the raft with lanyard as well, and keep it ready on the spray skirt, which lies across the raft's threshold. I make a sheath for the tip so that *Ducky*'s tubes will be safe even when the spear is picked up and thrown by the hands of the Atlantic.

Before I have time to test the new spear tip, the plug in the bottom tube trembles and little geysers shoot up at the bow. I put another tourniquet around the pads and plugs and twist it tight. A volcano of fat bubbles spews forth. She's blown again.

The still is also leaking more as my old repair works loose. I can't stop to reinflate the still when I am in the middle of lashing up the raft patch, so it slumps before I can get to it. The distillate becomes tainted with salt water. Just how tainted is hard to tell. I decide it is not *too* salty to drink, but as the salt level in my body builds, my ability to taste salt decreases. The fact that seawater is beginning to taste pretty fresh is frightening.

It is dusk when the patch blows, so I lie awake through the night with the tube deflated, huddling as close to the outside of *Ducky* as possible to keep from sagging too deeply into the floor. Cold and wet, I feel as if I'm lying in a hammock full of water, turned on its side. A heavy, rough lump brushes against me. Another shark. I grab my spear and try to maneuver for a shot. The squealing rubber floor sucks up my legs, twists, and tries to tear off my skin. I cannot see the shark, so try to pull my leggy lures out of the sea by sitting half up on the inflated tube with my head crammed against the canopy. Shivering, I await the dawn.

In every dusty corner of the attic of my mind, I search for a way to patch the leaking tube once and for all. The smaller line that I've been using for lashing rolls over itself too easily, until it rolls right off the end of the tear's puckered lips. Maybe if I use bigger line, it won't be able to roll over itself. I will grab just the tip of the puckered lips and wind the line so that the coils lie smoothly next to one another, spiraling like wire wound around a drum, pulling more and more of the lips under its control until the whole mouth of the tear is enclosed.

At daybreak I try this with quarter-inch line from the sea anchor. Thank God, it works.

Three hours later the whole thing blows.

I retie it, add some small-line tourniquets inboard of the large-line windings, and replace the external pressure-retaining lines. I pump up the tube until it is just hard enough to hold its shape.

Something beats monotonously at the floor. I sprawl across the top of *Ducky*'s canopy, crushing it down, and peer over the stern. I can feel that the rusty gas cylinder, which originally blew the raft up, has fallen out of its pouch. Not only is it good shark bait but its coarse metal may quickly scrape another hole in my ship. The wind has risen and waves slop over me as *Ducky* lifts and plunges like a pump diaphragm. I pull up on the gas line that connects the bottle to *Ducky*'s bottom tube. The gas bottle is heavy, full of water, I suppose, and refuses to be re-seated. The gas line has been pulled through the bottle's pocket so there's not enough slack to pull it up and out of the water. Can't get it back in and can't get it out, and I certainly can't leave it as is. Damn! I feel for the pocket and begin to slash away at it with my sheath knife, being very careful not to drop the blade or ram it into the tube. Twice a sharp pain runs up my arm. No matter. It's okay if I cut myself. Finally it's done, and I pull up the bottle and tie it to the upper tube.

My arms feel like lead, my whole body aches, and my head

feels as if it's been stuffed. For the past several days, I've had only a few hours' sleep and I've been sitting in salt water continually. Boils have burst open. Ulcers are growing. The hole that I rubbed through the skin of my left forearm while working on the patch has expanded, grown foul and smelly. I desperately need to satisfy the contradictory demands of food, water, and sleep—fish, navigate, tend the still, and keep watch until I drop. I get another trigger and devour the sour animal as if it were roast duck. The need to reinflate the raft again and again robs me of my sleep at night. There is no longer a clear line between good and evil, beauty and gruesomeness. Life is only one blurry moment following another deeper into fatigue and pain. I have become so conditioned to go through the motions of survival that I do them without thinking. It rains, and I leap to collect about six ounces of water, watching in disgust as small rivers pour into the mouth of the canopy, pure water turning instantly to bile.

The weather has been calm since the bottom tube was damaged. On the one hand, this has been fortunate because it has allowed me the time to evolve a patch. If a storm had hit when the bottom tube was deflated, I probably would have drowned, and almost certainly my equipment would have been torn out and washed away. As always, what's good on the one hand is bad on the other. In this period of calm, progress has been dreadfully slow. Recently the breeze has built—now to about twenty knots—and things are rough but not stormy. I'm glad the weather is back. At least we are moving again.

I have been too weak to do yoga for over a week. Before the accident, I thought I had reached a sort of starved, steady state, but now my body is becoming more battered and even thinner. I can take it. Others have taken worse. You're on the home stretch now, no letting up, push the pace. You've got to move even if you punch more holes in your hide, got to drive on. No second place in this race, only winning and losing. And we're not talking ribbons or trophies, here. You've got to hang in and be tough.

Will the seas punch the patch apart? Now, don't panic. DO NOT PANIC! Somehow I sleep. I dream that all of my family, friends, and those I've loved are gathered for a picnic. I try to take a picture of them sitting on a stone wall. Can't fit them all in. "You've got to get back," they shout to me. "Back, back, farther, keep going farther." I move back more and still more, bringing crowds into the frame. Thousands of speckles shout, "Back farther!" They shrink more, and still more sweep into view, until everyone turns to a blur and is gone.

The soggy floor of the raft is in such unbelievable motion it feels like a carnival ride. I can't imagine trying to effect another repair in these conditions. The patch splutters and spews, but it holds.

To protect the bow of the raft from my spear should another spear failure occur, and to prevent curious fish from nipping at the patch, I drape a bib of sailcloth through the entrance over the bow and let it drag under the raft. *Rubber Ducky III* has become a big-mouthed sea creature with a haggard tongue hanging out. I dangle inside like a weak tonsil. I pull the tongue tight against the raft so it does not flop, which would reduce my visibility and range for fishing. *Ducky* and I are now ready to gobble up anything in our path.

The farther west we get, the more we feel the effects of the warm, moist easterly trade winds. Cauliflower cumulus begin to sprout from the fertilized sky. Small showers fall in gray smudged streaks. I remove the kite that I'd originally made as a signaling device but ended up using to catch water that comes through the leaky observation port. I replace it with a plastic bag, which serves the purpose temporarily but not very efficiently. As the rain comes down, I hold the kite up like a shield against the drops, with the point down in the Tupperware box. The added square footage allows me to catch almost a pint of the sky's elixir.

For days the butcher shop's cupboards have been bare of any fresh food. Only a few dried fish sticks remain. They seem fine, even though they've hung for a month. The rock-hard amber sticks sit in my mouth for a half hour before they soften enough to be at all chewable.

Two Beatles songs begin to plague me, rolling around in my head again and again. Like the first song says, I am so very tired, and my mind is definitely on the blink. Okay, sure, why not just get up and fix myself a drink? Drink . . . drink . . . Humph. As if in answer to my frustration, the second song bursts out. Help! Yeah, sure, I need somebody, but I'd settle for *anybody*. Yes, I sure could use someone's—oh, universe, do you hear me?—Help! None comes, of course, no drink either; but the songs won't stop.

Food dreams become more real than ever. Sometimes I can smell the food; once I even tasted a dream. But it is always without substance. Even in reality, after I eat I am still hungry.

Once again I try for a dorado. I must be more particular than ever about my shot. The knives are too frail to drive through a fish at any angle or through its muscular back. I must somehow get off a gut shot. These piscatorial targets sometimes move at over thirty miles an hour, and I must hit a bull's eye of a few square inches. It seems beyond my feeble powers. However, the dorados have slowly developed identifiable styles of bumping *Rubber Ducky*. Some still stiffly punch the bottom or whack the perimeter with their tails, but some rub their sides against me, sliding against my knees and out in front of me on their sides. I am so close that I can see details of their eyes, tiny scars, and their pinprick nostrils.

Knives flash in the sunlight. *Ducky* makes rubbery groans, as if frightened. I spread out the sailcloth, sleeping bag, and cushion to protect as much of the raft as possible, particularly the tubes. I fire and hit a dorado perfectly under the spinal column, a large hole through her. I grab the spear with my left arm and lift the thrashing fish from the sea, keeping the point high in the air. I frantically try to pin her down on my sleeping bag. By the time my knife cracks her back, fish eggs and blood are spewed everywhere. So what? I have food! I make little hobbling jumps and yell, "Food! Food!"

My improvised spear works. I can rebuild my strength. *Ducky* is moving well and her patch is holding. With the stores in hand, I can last at least eight and maybe fifteen days. I'm being used up, but these past few minutes have given me a second wind . . . or is it an eighth or ninth? A month and a half ago I thought my chances were one in millions, yesterday less than one in ten. Now they're fifty-fifty.

From lessons learned while cleaning the triggers, I discover new areas of meat in the head of the dorado. More important are the new wells of fluid, from the fatty liquid eye sockets to the mucous deep in the gill cavity. By the time I throw out the skull, the bone is scraped clean. The stomach is greatly distended. I cut it out, carefully drain the stomach juices overboard, slit it open, and find that it is full of prey. A huge fish lies lodged from the back of the mouth to the top of the intestine. It's incredible that the dorado could have swallowed something that large. It would be easier to believe someone had ramrodded it down her throat. I wash it in the ocean. Only the skin has been digested. The dark meat is only slightly tangy and tastes quite like mackerel. I think of it as having been pickled. What a bonus. An extra pound of flesh. Two complete table settings of organs, including the eggs. I feel full for the first time in a month. This good fortune comes at a critical time. I have desperately needed a break. I feel as if this fish is a good omen, just as I felt the killing of the big dorado that I lost was a bad omen. Last time the omen proved valid. I hope that this time it will too, that things will now brighten up.

By now the habitat in which I live, Duckyville, has become a neighborly suburb. The fish and I are familiar so I can chat with them individually, spread gossip and rumor. I recognize a dorado's nudge, a trigger's peck, or a shark's scrape the way you recognize different neighbors' knocks on the back door. Often I know which individual fish is whacking the raft with its tail or butting it with its head. I can tell when the fish are around even when they don't knock or flap. I love my little friends and their tight little town. No plague of politics, ambition, or animosity. Simple, unmysterious, unapprehensive life.

But there is a mystery in this town nonetheless. I failed at catching the dorados by line and they came close enough for the spear. The range of the spear was shortened when I lost the power strap, but they bumped and swam even closer. Now, with my range shortened even more and my power declining, they lie on their sides under my point. It is as if they are trying to help me, as if they do not mind mixing their flesh with mine.

High in the sky, long, thin, highly arched wings trail a delicate forked tail. Frigate birds do not venture so far from land, do not sleep at sea, and do not fish for themselves; or at least that is what I have read. Yet the shape of the bird—its pointed wings locked into position, its slim body and tail—certainly fits the description. I am still six hundred miles out, and the bird appears to be eyeing the same flying fish on which the dorados feed.

Night comes, and the weather turns more foul. I hear the patch bubbling and seething as the bow dips and rises in the waves. Pumping more frequently, now every half hour, I realize that I will not last long with such a workload.

Whitecaps occasionally break upon the canopy and crash through the opening about my head. Quarts of water drain down over me. The raft lurches up and down, so I hang on to the handline with one hand, just in case *Ducky* is knocked down again. I can't possibly sleep, so I calmly await the warming sun. Suddenly loud flaps rattle the canopy just above my head. I leap out and hijack the flying fish before it has a chance to flop back off into the sea. As sunlight peeks into *Ducky*, I clean my beautiful catch. A flyer's head is shaped in cross section like an upside-down triangle. Huge eyes look down and to each side to keep predators in sight while the flyer glides over the water. I scrape the large round scales off of her flat indigo back and slender white stomach and then remove her long translucent wings. The tail blades form a V aft, and the bottom one sweeps down almost twice as long as the top. Flyers can soar over a hundred yards, and by flicking this little rudder they can get some extra yardage or change direction. Blind flight at night sometimes carries a whole school straight into the side of a passing boat; when they hit, it sounds like machine-gun fire. A number of times, late at night or early in the morning, I have been jolted awake by a painful direct hit in the chest or the face. The flyers' tasty flesh is soft and pinkish white.

At first light, I spot a frigate bird overhead. So much for the idea that they never spend a night at sea. It sits almost motionless, as if painted there.

Warmth never comes. The sun remains hidden, the black waves break noisily all around me. I would like to remain wrapped up in my sleeping bag, but a wave crashes against the bow, and even above the terrible racket of the tumultuous sea, I hear a hissing eruption. *Ducky*'s bottom tube becomes flaccid, the floor bubbles up, and we settle again deep in the water. It's no use bailing. The top tube gives only a few inches of freeboard. Water flows in and out of my territory at will.

The entire foam plug has been shot out of the hole. I must sew it in place and try once more to relieve the pressure that tries to pull the tear's lips out flat. Since the shortest distance between two points is a straight line, I decide to warp the shape of the raft so that, when viewed from above, it will look like a doughnut with a bite taken out of one side. I tie long lines across the bow from one handline anchor point to another, then tighten the lines by twisting them until they pull the raft into the warped shape. Next I string a line from bow to stern on the inside and pull until the raft folds up in half. This lifts the bow enough that I can see the tear. With my awl I cut small holes in the lips of the tear and the foam plug. I force through codline and tie the plug in place. As I have done so many times before, I lash it up, add external pressure lines, tourniquets, the works.

When *Ducky* is afloat again, I can still hear a high whistle of escaping air echoing through her tubes.

Again the night is miserable. Choppy six- to ten-foot seas are on the attack. The canopy dribbles its sour water over me. Intense, stabbing pain from salt water sores mixes with throbbing aches that run through my muscles.

At 9:00 A.M. the patch blows again. The stock of dorados droops against the wet floor of the raft, turning rancid. Hundreds of sores now fester and eat into my nerves, more breaking and oozing each hour. I've slept for only four hours or less each night of the past week, eaten less than two pounds of food a day, and worked almost nonstop. I'm beginning to panic.

MARCH 27
DAY 51

Got to stop it! I've got to get it sealed! Can't. Arms too tired to move. Shut up! Got to. No choice. Move, arms, move! I try to order my beaten and bedraggled body back into action. I crawl forward, relash the patch. She blows. I lash it again. She blows! Time and again the sea throws the raft down. Water smashes against me, flinging me into the torrent that sloshes in and out. Stabbing spasms, twinging, throbbing, convulsive cramping, piercing pain. I cannot take it, I won't make it. Stop it! *Harder, got* to pull the strings tighter. Got to try. World is reeling. Words echoing. Forgotten memories. Hands trembling, skin breaking. Pull harder, *harder!* Groaning, gasping. *Pump.* How many? Don't know, can't count. Three hundred maybe. Top tube, too, another ninety. My arms are being torn from their sockets, and I am being flayed alive. A wave crashes in. My world jumps and shakes. She blows. Tie her up again, *harder.* Get it to stick. The still hangs lifeless over the bow. Pump up the tube. So long, now, ever so long. Two hundred eighty. Rest. O.K., squeeze. Two eighty-one . . . She blows!

Collapse, can't move. My left arm is searing. With my right, I drag it up onto my chest. Night is here. So very cold, but I do not shiver. I'm lifeless, floating like a wet rag along the top of the sea. Can't move any more. Numb. The end is come.

Breathing hard. Gasping! Yes, I guess I am. Eight days I've been trying to patch the leak. No more, please, no more. The ocean rolls me about, sloshes over me, beats me, but I do not resist, hardly feel it. Tired, so very tired. Heaven, Nirvana, Moksa . . . where are they? Can't see them, don't feel them. Only the dark. Is this illusion or real? Aah, word games of the religious and philosophical. Words aren't real. Hours? Yes. Fifty-one days gone and some hours left. I've stumbled, fallen, lost. Why, why, why? Eternity? Yes, the ocean rolls on. I roll on. No. Not I. Carbon, water, energy, love. They go on. Skin and bones of the universe, of God, flexing, always moving. I am lost, lost without trace.

An immense energy pulls at my mind, as if I am imploding within my body. A dark pit widens, surrounding me. I'm frightened, so frightened. My eyes well with tears, pulling me away from the emptiness. Sobbing with rage, pity, and self-pity, clawing at the slope, struggling to crawl out, losing grip, slipping deeper. Hysterical wailing, laments, lost hope. I scrape to catch hold of something, but nothing is there. Darkness widening, closing in. How many eyes have seen like mine? I feel them, all around me, millions of faces, whispering, crowding in, calling, "Come, it is time."

TWICE TO HELL AND BACK

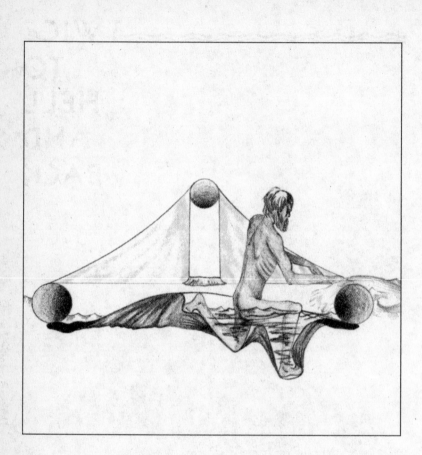

reach from the darkness and pull me down. I'm
falling. It's come.

"No!" I yell out. "Can't! Won't!" Can't let go. Tears stream down my face and mix with the sea swilling around my body. Will die, and soon . . . Find the answer. Want to . . . yes! That's it, want to live. Despite agony and horror. Despite what lies ahead. I convulse, sobbing, "I want to LIVE, to LIVE to LIVE!"

Can't.

Must! Damn it, open your eyes. They blink, heavy with fatigue. Try to focus.

Not good enough.

Quit your bitching! Do it! Grab ahold, arms. PUSH! Now again, PUSH! Good. Up a bit. Won't drown now. Breath is heavy. O.K., steady, boy. Head sways, eyes blur. A wave comes in. Cool. Keep your own cool, too. Stop that whining! Get that bag over you. Do it! All right. Rest now. You're out of it, for now. You're O.K. You hear me?

Yes.

O.K.

Now what? Next time it won't be so easy.

Shut up! You've got to come up with something. Got to get warm, got to rest, got to think. Maybe one chance left. Maybe not even that. It's got to work first time. If it doesn't, you WILL DIE! *Will Die*, Will Die, will die. Yes. I must make this one good.

Go back. Identify the problem. Use what you've learned.

My mind wanders, coherent at times, then stumbling like a drunk into a babbling stupor. Die, lost without trace . . . The ultimate question, death . . . Damn it, concentrate! O.K. Old problem: plug coming out. Solved by sewing it in. Current problem: lashings working off. I have to keep them on. What equipment have I got? Space blanket, flare gun, useless lighter, plastic bag. Maybe I can pull the bottom of the raft tight by yanking up on the bottom tube all around and tying it to the upper tube. Not much better than what I've done before, and it's too complicated. I'll have to cut holes in the bottom tube; but then there's no going back. The answer has to be simpler. What else have I got? First aid kit, bandages, scissors, twine, line. And all the stuff I've already used—spoon, fork, radar refl . . . The fork! Of course! Why you stupid bloody idiot! "It's the fork!"

Adrenalin begins to surge through my veins. Like magic, I get the strength to bundle up and try to regain my lost body heat. I eat whatever fish is in sight, wait, and plan. I lie awake all night planning. Every detail is considered, every contingency followed to its possible conclusion. I don't know if I'll last the night, but there is nothing to do but try. I huddle up, try to stay away from cold spots in the raft, places that have not been warmed by my body. At last my eyes can tell gray from black, and then orange from gray.

I throw off my covers and feel the cold morning breeze on my skin. With my sheath knife, I carefully cut a slit through the top lip, foam tongue, and bottom lip of the tear. I break the tines off of the fork and slip the handle through the slit so that it sticks out of both sides like a bone through a cannibal's nose. Conveniently, there are two holes in the handle, just to the top and bottom of the lips. I can lash across the patch and through the holes to keep the handle snugly in position. The line that I wind behind the handle cannot be forced off unless the handle breaks. First I use a light line to grab the middle of the lips and pinch them tight onto the tongue. Then I coil the thicker line around until it winds the lips back into a pucker and ultimately encloses the outside edges of the mouth. I know this thicker line is not effective in making the patch airtight. Its only purpose is to lie smoothly next to itself and pucker the lips. For the final seal, I loop a tourniquet behind the coil of thicker rope and wring it tight. The thicker rope will keep the tourniquet from rolling off the edges of the mouth when the tube is inflated.

I must rest between each step of the operation, so it takes until midafternoon. When it is finished, I begin pumping up the tube, taking a half hour to do what would normally take five minutes. After an hour and a half, the reinflated tube is quite soft again. I'm depressed, but as long as I have strength I must try to make it work. There is no other answer.

The fork handle has kept the lashings on the top and bottom of the lips, but the two edges to the sides have bulged out just enough that a trickle of air escapes. I pull the lines back down over the sides, using warping lines, attachment points on the top tube, and whatever else I can think of. I give the tourniquet a few more cranks and add a second one. Time to give it another go. By now I whine more than the pump. In the hour that follows, *Ducky* gorges on air, picks herself out of the water, and drifts forward again like a lily pad cut free from its roots. I collapse into a heap of human rubble.

Twelve glorious hours pass before *Ducky* needs another feeding. Her lips have ceased to regurgitate the three hundred mouthfuls of air every few hours. I pump in only thirty little bites and her belly is as plump as a melon again. The gray sky and tormented sea continue to cast a pall over my surroundings. My body hungers, thirsts, and is in constant pain. But I feel great! I have finally succeeded!

The night I lost *Solo* and again last evening, there seemed no escape from death: it could come at any moment. The first time, over a week passed before I became accustomed to the raft and saw that there was a possibility that I might get enough food and water to crawl out of this hell hole. This time it was much worse. After the bottom tube was punctured, my life in the raft was more horrible than I could have imagined early in the voyage. I feel as though I have been twice to hell and back, and each successive journey has taken longer, been more hopeless and abominable. I will never last another one. Even now I wonder if I will be able to recover enough strength to last three or more weeks, long enough to reach the islands. I must be positive about it. I must regain a firm and unquestioned com-

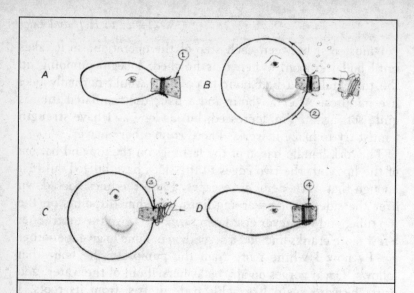

E V O L U T I O N   O F   T H E   P A T C H   I N   T H E   B O T T O M   T U B E.
(A) The tear is like a mouth. I push a foam plug (1) into the
mouth and wind lashings around the lips. From a top view the
edges of the mouth would be barely enclosed by the lashings.
(B) When the tube is inflated, it pulls the lips apart (2). They
work out from under the lashings, the lashings and foam plug
fall out, and the tube again deflates. (C) Holes are punched
through the lips and plug and it is "sewn" into place (3). However, when the tube is inflated, the lips are again pulled apart
and the small diameter line rolls over itself and again falls off.
(D) I wind a larger diameter line around the lips (4). This keeps
the smaller line inboard of it. However, when the tube is inflated,
the same problem occurs. The lips are pulled apart and both the
large and small diameter lines are forced off of the plug. I use
extra line to tie the large diameter line to various tie-down points
on the raft. However, they are not numerous enough or close
enough to the patch to be totally effective. They keep the lines
from completely falling off, but the edges of the lips still pull
out from under the lashings no matter how tightly they are wound
around the mouth. (E) The normal raft shape as viewed from
above, and how I warp it in order to gather more of the lips

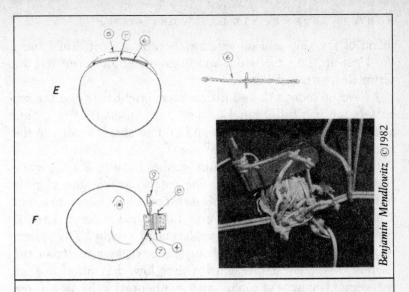

Benjamin Mendlowitz ©1982

around the plug. Dotted line (5) shows the raft's normal, circular shape. By using a loop of line, twisted in Spanish windlass style (6), two anchor points on the raft are pulled together. This allows the mouth to be slightly puckered even when the raft is reinflated (7). (F) The final, primary patching system. (External pressure patches and lines tying the various lines to anchor points on the raft are also necessary to make the patch effective but are not shown here, for clarity.) A fork handle (8) is inserted down through the top lip, plug, and bottom lip. This keeps the lashings from being forced off the end of the patch. The large line (4) is wound around until all edges of the mouth are caught. Then small diameter line is wound tightly around in order to apply pressure on the lips against the plug. Finally, a tourniquet (9) is used to maximize pressure on the plug. This keeps the edges of the mouth that are perpendicular to the fork handle from pulling out from under the lashings and it cinches the patch so tightly that it finally holds air better than the undamaged top tube. PHOTOGRAPH OF THE FINAL PATCH. Tie-downs to a nearby anchor point and to the warping Spanish windlass (7) can be seen running under the patch. The metal pintle serves to tighten the tourniquet and is also lashed into place.

mand of my ship and myself, for there is a great deal I must do. I get up, face the wind, and in no uncertain terms tell the Grim Reaper to get lost!

I have no more fish and little water. Night falls and the sea batters me painfully, but I cannot stay conscious. I rest, find sleep, await the sun's return, and ever so slowly return to the land of the living.

On our fifty-third day, the sun brushes the clouds aside while the wind pushes us onward. The patch has loosened slightly but has held. I feel as if I've been run over by a locomotive, but I have more confidence than ever that I will make it. Even if the patch fails, I can make a replacement rapidly. The system works. My position is still about three weeks away from the islands. My body has reached a new low, has no chance to recover and no hope of coping with another major disaster. From here on it will be a full-time struggle to hang on to but not break the thread that connects me to my world.

At the beginning of my voyage, there was little distinction between my rational mind and the rest of me. My emotions were ruled by nearly instinctive training and my body did not complain about having to work. But the distinction between the parts of myself continues to grow sharper as the two-edged sword of existence cuts one or another of them more deeply each day. My emotions have been stressed to the point of breaking. The smallest things set me into a rage or a deep depression, or fill me with overwhelming compassion, especially for my fish. My body is now so beaten that it has trouble following my mind's commands. It wants only to rest and find relief from the pain. But rationally I have chosen not to use my first aid kit because it is small and I may need it more later if I am severely injured. Each decision like this by my mind comes at an increasing cost to the rest of my crew. I must coerce my emotions to kill in order to feed my body. I must coerce my arms and legs to perform in order to give myself a feeling of hope. I try to comply with contradictory demands, but I know the other parts of me have bent to my cold, hard rationalism as best they can. I am slowly losing the ability to command, and if it goes, I am lost. It becomes a problem that surpasses the constant apprehension of living on the edge. I carefully watch for signs of mutiny within myself.

For the first time, I try to dry out my sleeping bag by draping it over the canopy of the raft. Heavy with water, it crushes the canopy. I pump up the arch tube as tightly as possible. It's all my rubbery legs can do to support me for the minutes it takes to maneuver the bag and tie it down to keep it from flying away. The inside of my cave is now dimmer and cooler, an advantage as the sun reaches its zenith. Despite occasional spray rewetting the bag, by nightfall it is mostly dry. Each evening, though, dampness from the air is drawn into the salt-encrusted seams.

The still is not functioning properly. The cloth wick is not getting as wet as it should. Evidently the valve is plugged. A jiggle string passes through the valve to regulate flow. It's stuck, and after some tight maneuvers I manage to free it with the tweezers from the first aid kit. Time and time again the jiggle string becomes relodged. I lash my only safety pin onto a pencil and bend the point out straight. I must be very careful not to puncture the balloon. I maneuver the prong down through the valve to free it. This still deflates each night. At dawn I inflate it, empty it of salt water, and prime it up. All day I nurse it, feed it salt water, operate on the valve seizures, and maintain the perfect level of inflation. I must doctor the still constantly, and in return the still nurses my feeble form with fresh liquid.

The sun climbs up to its throne. Beads of silver slowly grow on the inside of the balloon and eventually they drop down, leaving black streaks as they roll along the inside of the balloon's surface, collecting the silver condensation as they go. My eyes are heavy. The monotonous progression of waves drones a chant of rolling lullabies, and the slow drip, drip, drip . . . My eyes open with a start. How long have I slept? Half hour, maybe. The still, too, has slumped over. I grab the collection bag. Much too full. Damn! Contaminated with seawater again. Chalk off another six ounces of good water. From now on I'll empty the bag every hour or more. The forced activity will help to keep me from lapsing into sleep. Two tropic birds flap by in their awkward way, hiding behind their black masks and laughing at me. I don't find it very funny. I prop the still back up and get it to sweat. Gnawing on a triggerfish fillet, I discover that they don't taste so bad if dried a little.

Yesterday I began the hunt again. The doggies seemed to know I was back in the game. As my point neared the water surface, their groups burst apart and scattered. I couldn't hold my hunting position for long, but the triggers underestimated me. They must have thought that I'd have packed it in by sunset. I ground my teeth in the shadows and stabbed one, then another. Two clicking bodies lay before me. I ripped into the first like a werewolf, and after licking the remaining strands of flesh and guts off of my beard I felt much revived. The second I stretched out on my board and dissected under the beam of my flashlight, which I held in my mouth. I tossed the flesh into the Tupperware box and fell asleep. I woke toward midnight and found an eerie aura casting shadows. The Tupperware box was glowing. I drew back the top and saw the dead meat alive with light. Phosphorescent plankton, which lodge in the weeds and barnacles on which the trigger feeds, must have found their way into the fish's flesh. The light from their microscopic lives illuminates my world long after they have died.

This morning, finishing the last of the trigger, I am aware once again that I do not know where my next meal will come from. We overtake some large clumps of sargasso, which are no longer pristine and newly sprouted as they were far to the east. From the feathery branches I shake tiny shrimp, a half-inch-long fish, and a number of thick black worms bristling with white spines. I do not touch the worms. Chris made that mistake when we sailed to England, and he was left with a fistful of glasslike barbed slivers. I pick through the weed, searching for the small crabs, which try to scurry from my grasp. I collect them, pinching their shells so that they do not suffer long and do not escape.

Potbellied, mottled-skinned sargasso fish up to an inch long also fall out of the weed. I don't know that they are inedible, but I do find them very bitter. They do not taste too bad if I am careful not to eat their bloated bellies. And what are these gelatinous little slugs? They have four flipperlike jelly legs and a greenish and salty tasting body. I save the crabs and shrimp for dessert. Sometimes when I pop a crab into my mouth before killing it, the wee claws give my cheeks or tongue a little pinch, which makes me conscious of the small life I am taking.

In the early evening, rain clouds streak across the heavens, raising my hopes that I can rebuild my water stock. A light drizzle wets everything inside, since the canopy is now about as waterproof as a T-shirt. Early in the morning the drops fatten and strike with a tap, first one, a pause, then twenty, like spilled ball bearings, a pause, then a stampede of hard round bullets. I lunge for my kite and hold it out. The rain splatters on the Tupperware and off of the still. I'm able to collect ten ounces of good clear water and lick the residue of drops from the still. I feel quenched and confident again. By day's end my water supply will be completely replenished.

As I reseat myself on my cushion and flip the sleeping bag over my legs, I notice a small fin protruding from a crevice between my equipment bag and the raft's tubes. The rain has brought me an added reward. A large flying fish has lost its way in the downpour, brushed by me unnoticed, and crashed inside. While I await dawn, a small hurricane rattles the canopy and another flyer becomes lodged on the tent. After I have eaten the savory flesh of this flyer, I push the remaining head and tail together to see how they look. Not bad, not bad at all. I dig out my fishing gear and push the shank of a large treble hook from the back of the head out of the mouth of the flyer. I push the tail over the barbs of two large single hooks that I tie together, and then string these to the shank of the treble hook, using heavy sail twine. With the tail joined to the head this way, I've created a very short specimen of flying fish. The lure is so convincing that I'm tempted to bite it myself.

Fishing for dorados without wire leader is a pointless exercise, but it has dawned on me that there may be a strand of wire on the radar reflector. As I unroll the greased paper, a spidery web of Monel mesh and aluminum struts is revealed. The sea has also invaded here and has caused metallic sores. Electrolytic corrosion has eaten gaping, encrusted ulcers through the aluminum struts. However, there is a strong piece of stainless-steel wire, about eighteen inches long. I take note of the other valuable bits of metal and fasteners and pack the reflector away again.

The dorados have recently been shy of my spear, but they seem particularly voracious. I cast out a bit of trigger offal, and they leap upon it like frenzied sharks. I fling my lure out and work it aft, thirty feet, fifty feet, a hundred. I see it wiggling just under the crystal surface. A flash of indigo and snow whips by in front of it. The strike is hard. A jerk, another jerk, and then nothing. I watch the dorado dart off into the distance.

He has struck at the head of the lure. It seems that dorados often eat their meals head first, at least judging from the remains that I've taken from their stomachs. I have often noticed that the dorados travel in male-female pairs. I now believe that the pairing may serve more than one purpose. Perhaps one fish herds prey into the jaws of a companion who waits in the prey's path. If the herding dorado can catch the flyer from behind, so much the better for him or her. I can only make wild guesses about the dorados' behavior because I can observe them only when they are near me, a hundred feet away at most. If only I could swim with them to study the intricacies of their private lives.

I reset my lure with the remaining flying fish head. This time I'll give it enough slack to be swallowed. The dorado soon approaches. I give a few feet of line, stalling the midget flyer. He swallows. Take it in, deeply now. I yank to set the hook. Got him! The dorado thrashes forward as if engaging afterburners, flips his head, neatly bites the line off just ahead of the wire, and is gone. I will never catch a dorado by line. I must return to the spear.

The lure that I make from a flying fish is so
convincing I'm tempted to bite it myself.

I figure I'm about 450 miles from Antigua. Could be off 100 miles either way, maybe more. Another eighteen days. Humph. At the beginning of this voyage, eighteen days was too much to ask for. Now I demand it.

As my equipment continues to wear out and break, and as my living corpse of a body continues to decompose, I must try harder to prepare for every eventuality. Only a few flares left. Well past the lanes. The islands still a long way off. But I'm too close now and have come through too much to let go.

At dusk in lumpy seas I spear a female dorado. In the course of the melee, the sun sinks, and a pool of ocean flows around my knee. Somehow the spear tip has pierced the floor. It's too small a slit to fit a plug into, so I take my knife out and increase the damage. No sweat. It's big enough now to ram a plug in, screw tight, and bind up with codline. Why, looky there, doesn't even leak a drop, even pulls the baggy floor a little tighter. I should have done this to the other holes in the bottom, and will if the patches come off again.

Inside the dorado is another mackerel-like fish, though smaller and more digested than the last. I can't get the flashlight to work, so I break out one of my two Lumalights. When the light stick is bent, two chemicals mix and give off a greenish glow. Rich fare is spread out on the board before me: two livers, a sac of eggs, two kinds of meat, and a full half pint of water. I eat by green candlelight. Things are looking up.

Showers come in the night and soak everything, but I only collect a little water. A ship heading west passes too far away to see my next-to-last parachute flare. A month ago I would have fired off three or more flares, but now I am much more realistic. I'll wait for a ship that is in a better position to see me. I can't afford to waste flares. Besides, I am getting very confident, perhaps too confident, that if a ship does not pick me up I will still make it to the islands. The overcast morning ruins my chances of distilling water, but I remain undaunted. Here's a breakfast fit for King Kong: huge steaks, a quarter pound of eggs, hearts, eyes, and a scraping of fat. Yum!

I'm in pretty warm waters now. Even if I get soaked, I'm not going to die of hypothermia overnight. Rain, at least a light shower, is becoming an almost daily occurrence. The space blanket can be risked for other purposes. I turn it into a water collection cape for the back of the canopy, rolling the edges to act like gutters. It's wide at the top, along the canopy arch tube, and funnels to a point, which I drag through the leaky observation port. Any waves sloshing over the canopy, as well as any rain, will now pour in as if through an open faucet. However, the back of the canopy is so leaky now that water pours in from all over. The cape covers most of the aft side, which is more weathered and less waterproof than the front. It makes the back a lot drier, though rain and spray still make their way around and under the cape. The cape catches about sixty to seventy percent of the water and drains it down through the faucet, so it is much easier to catch than when it poured in at random. I can hang the Tupperware box under the tap and bail it out with my coffee can, or I can put the can directly under the tap.

As I pick through more seaweed, a fish, too thin to be a dorado but of the same length, flits across my peripheral vision. Twice now I've gotten a glance of this fish. A barracuda? A shark? It's not important. What is important is that there are new species in my world. Something is happening. I can feel it, like a scout who feels the warmth of ashes and knows how recently men sat around the campfire.

New bird life shows its wings. In the distance, two birds fight. Perhaps they are gulls, but more likely they're terns. One of the charts from Robertson's book shows that the migration path of terns crosses my approximate position.

Sometimes you can use techniques that were developed by the South Seas islanders to tell if there is land ahead. You look for such indications as wave formations as they hit a shore and bounce back out to sea, rising cumulus clouds that skyrocket to great heights from thermal currents over the land, phosphorescent lines in the water at night, and so forth. I haven't detected any of these things. The most reliable method is to see land

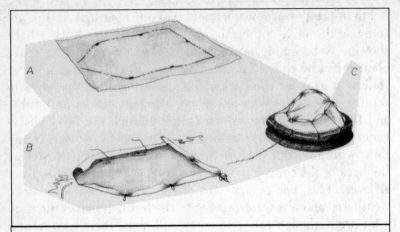

I make a water collection cape from the remaining part of the space blanket (part of the blanket I used previously to make a kite). (A) I plan out the shape and poke "buttonholes" in the blanket, through which I can thread twine to tie it up and to act as anchoring points. (B) I roll the sides to act like gutters, directing most of the water down to the apex of the point to the left. In the point I tie in a piece of tubing to act as a drain. I will pull this apex and drain through the observation port on the back of the raft. I can then direct the drain into a water container. Through the buttonholes, I tie string, and each knot is fitted with a loop to which I attach lanyards that run down to the raft's exterior handline. (C) The water collection cape is shown in position, with the point pulled through the observation port, the lanyards pulling it down and spreading it out as much as possible, and the top gutter lying along the ridge of the arch tube.

itself. But sighting land from a distance is always a tricky problem. When clouds are above you, they appear to move quickly. But as they near the horizon, you look through the atmosphere at an oblique angle and the clouds appear to move slower and slower while they also become darker. Cumulus clouds take on the illusory form of high volcanic rims or low, flat islands. Some remain still for so long that you begin to believe they are solid earth. Only by very long observation can the sailor distinguish land from clouds.

When Chris and I were approaching the Azores, I sighted a light gray conical shape among the high, fluffy cumulus. It did not move for several hours, slowly grew more distinct, and then extended itself down. We had sighted Faial from forty miles out, while the lower parts of the island were hidden in white haze at sea level. On the other hand, I once was less than a mile from thousand-foot cliffs in the Canaries on a sunny, clear day, when the sun illuminated some haze and the whole island disappeared. I desperately hope that I have underestimated my speed and that of the current. I've tried to be conservative. I watch for a stable form at the horizon, one that will stay put and turn green, but each shape I see slowly transforms itself into a winged horse or angel and flies off beyond sight.

It is the end of March. Will April showers bring May flowers, or will the first of April be a cosmic joke? Thought you'd make it, did you? Well, April fool!

Clouds drop a light shower to test my water-catchment system. I get about a pint, but upon tasting it I find that it's still badly tainted with foul orange particles from the canopy. My catchment cape isn't as effective as I had hoped. There's still too much water draining down the canopy. This foul water drains through the same hole in the canopy as the clean water from the catchment cape. Maybe the foul water will be drinkable if I cut it with good water. I try a fifty-fifty ratio. It's still so gross that it's all I can do not to barf. Maybe if I cut it again with water from the still . . .

APRIL 1
DAY 56

The sun peers out from behind the wall of gray and sets the solar still to working. Dancing droplets pirouette into the collection bag. The still keeps slumping over. The hole in its skirt must be getting critically large. I have to blow it up every ten or fifteen minutes. Production seems good, too good. I try to ignore the fact that the distilled water is growing salty. I'm dreadfully thirsty. The sea itself isn't so bad. If I mix the salty distilled water with the tainted fresh water, that should help dilute both the salt and the wretched flavor. When I get it all mixed together, I have a concoction that would be a fitting test of manhood in any ancient tribal ritual, a mix of water, rock salt, and vomit. Get rid of it. Don't want to pollute tomorrow's water production, but can't afford to throw it out. I hold my nose and swallow. The liquid slightly burns as I gulp it down.

Off of Puerto Rico, the ship *Stratus* sights a small boat adrift. *Stratus* reports to the Coast Guard, which asks for a description of the derelict vessel. It does not fit *Solo's* description. By day's end, the Coast Guard notifies my family that the "search" for me has ended. They do not mention the *Stratus*. My brother Ed has been calling my parents daily to see if there has been any word from me. He is frustrated by the lack of information from official sources. Either they are not telling everything they know, or they are not conducting a very extensive search. Ed leaves his home in Hawaii and boards a plane for Boston, where he joins my parents and brother Bob. They will conduct their own search-and-rescue mission.

In the dark, I cannot sleep. The wretched water sloshes about in my gut like a heavy stone. My head begins to ache and sweat. My neck tightens, and I feel pressure like a thumb rammed up under my jaw. Nausea sweeps over me. My pulse races, my head throbs. By midnight, steamy sweat rolls off my hot skin, and I roll back and forth in anguish. My God, I have poisoned myself.

ROAD
OF
TRASH

EACH BUBBLE AND RIPPLE has been frozen in white ice streaming down over the precipice like the long frosty beard of Old Man Winter. The motion of the torrent is stopped, awaiting the thaw of spring. Within the frigid shell, the waterfall continues to thunder downward, splashing up into my glass, which rattles with stark blue shards of ice. The sparkling, effervescent liquid is held toward my lips, but my swooning head keeps dropping back from it. I open my eyes so I do not have to look at it any more.

Nausea strangles me. My tongue feels like a toad in my mouth. I can stand it no longer. Desperately I pull out a pint of my precious reserve, unscrew the cap, and pull on the bag. The water sits in my cheeks for a moment before I push my toady tongue upward and squirt it down my throat in an effort to douse the blaze in my belly. Another mouthful. The conflagration flickers. Another, then another. The pint bag hangs flaccid. The pyromaniac surrenders. Nausea is drowned. I sleep.

In the morning I am weak, but I am able to catch my eleventh triggerfish and refortify myself with its fresh organs and with sticks of dorado. I am back in the battle.

Sticky gum has separated and clotted on the back of the remaining remnants of repair tape. I scrape up a small ball of gum with my knife and push a little plug of the goop through the hole in the solar still. I squish it over on both sides like a rivet. With the piece of repair tape wedged in over the gooey rivet, the replaced patch is markedly improved, gives my lungs a furlough, and keeps the blasted salt in the ocean where it belongs.

APRIL 2
DAY 57

There's no telling how long the still will last. Buddha's bellybutton is getting bigger. I'd better collect and store as much water as I can now. The ballast ring from the cut-up still makes

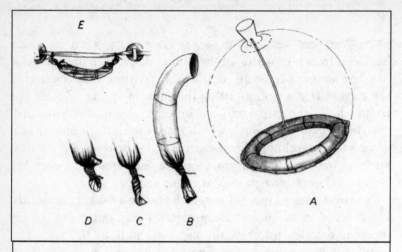

(A) I cut the ballast ring from the cut-up solar still. I slice this in half so that I can easily fill it through the open mouth on one end. (B) I tightly tie up one end, but it still leaks quite a lot so (C) I twist the tail and (D) pull it back upward and securely lash it up. Amazingly it still leaks, albeit at a very slow pace. After the container is filled, I repeat the closure process on the other end and (E) hang the container horizontally from the interior handline. This keeps the ends up and prevents leakage.

two decent containers. I cut it in half and bind up one end of each half. I can easily pour water into the open ends, which are about three inches in diameter, then lash them up. If it comes to it, I'll store tainted rainwater in these containers. The drainage tube may serve for administering a foul enema.

The wind is blowing us more northerly. Time to fix latitude. I lash three pencils into a triangle to make a low-budget sextant. Sextants are fancy protractors with mirrors that allow the navigator to look at the horizon and a star or planet at the same time. Early predecessors of the sextant include the cross-staff and backstaff made of wood. My instrument is even more primitive, since I cannot view both the stars and the horizon at the same time. Instead, I must move my head up and down, first viewing a star along one pencil and then the rim of the world along the other, while attempting to hold the instrument still. I will try it this evening.

Above Antigua the West Indies begin to bend off westward. If I drift above eighteen degrees latitude, I'll have to last another twenty or thirty days to reach the Bahamas. Guadeloupe is the most eastern island in the West Indies group. I'm aiming for seventeen degrees latitude. If a navigator stands on the North Pole, the North Star will sit directly overhead at ninety degrees to the horizon in all directions. The top of the world is at ninety degrees latitude. On the equator, at zero degrees latitude, Polaris dances right on the horizon. So latitude can be directly determined by the angle between the polestar and the horizon. I will try to measure the angle of the North Star to the horizon to give me my latitude.

Determining longitude is another matter entirely. To do so, the navigator equates arc with time. Each of the 360 degrees of the earth's circular belt line is divided into sixty minutes of arc. Each minute is one nautical mile—6076 feet. Since the earth spins once every twenty-four hours, the heavenly bodies pass over fifteen degrees of longitude every hour, or fifteen minutes of longitude every minute. Some astronomers in Greenwich, England, began and ended their demarcation of the globe by running the longitude line of zero degrees through their little town. Longitude can be calculated by comparing the time when a heavenly body appears overhead to the time when it would be over Greenwich. The difference in time is then converted to arc, which tells the observer how far east or west of Greenwich he is. Not until the advent of accurate timepieces was it possible to fix longitude.

Captain Cook was one of the first to utilize the breakthrough invention called the chronometer. Until then, mariners commonly sailed north or south until they reached the latitude on

Taking a sight with my pencil sextant

which their port of destination lay. Then they would sail directly east or west. Latitude sailing, as it is called, figured on the altitude of the North Star, combined with my approximate speed and drift, which I have been keeping running track of, will give me a better idea of my position in this expanse of terrain barren of signposts and landmarks.

I measure off eighteen degrees from the chart's compass rose and set my sextant at this angle. Go west, young *Ducky*, and south.

The dorados strike hard all day, irritating my sores and infuriating me. The sky is clear again, the afternoon hot. Light winds swing to the south and push us north. Oh, hell! All night brilliant moonlight illuminates at least a hundred triggerfish and thirty escorting dorados that continually smash into *Ducky*. We go due north, then northeast, then east, right where we came from. Damn!

By morning we've completed the loop and are back on course. I'm happy that my sextant says we're at seventeen degrees latitude, but it could be off by a degree or more. One degree the wrong way and I add a month to my trip. It's too close for comfort. And a day lost going nowhere. I can't expect consistent progress. Fifty-eight days, but I must be more patient and even more determined.

APRIL 3
DAY 58

Bubbles gurgle out from *Ducky*'s patch. I've got to pump every hour and a half to keep the tube tight. I tighten the tourniquet around the neck of the patch. The line struggles and then explodes, but the patch remains generally in place. I whip a noose of stronger cord around and pull it tight. Miraculously the bottom tube now holds air better than the top.

A number of dorados nudge my butt. They'll stick around for a while. Good time for a shot. I aim and fire. Miss. Again. Hit. A fine female. Lifted up, she glints in the sun. Her body pulses. She curls her head toward her tail—left side, right side, left, right, faster and faster. My delicate lance sways to her rhythm.

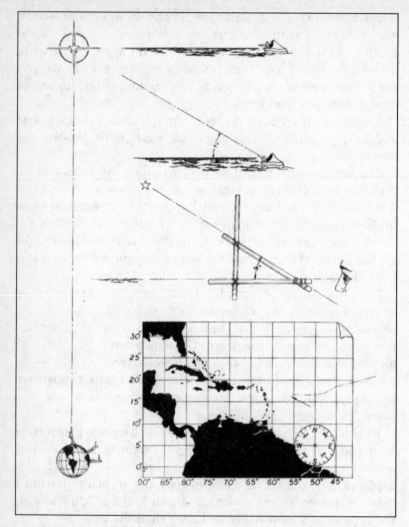

What a magnificent animal. In one smooth move that has become instinctive, I swing her inside and finish her off. Again I am provided with a buffer against starvation. Again I'm saddened by the loss of a companion. More and more I feel that these creatures exude a spirit that dwarfs mine. I don't know how to

BASIC NAVIGATION. My position east-west was estimated by my speed of drift added to the approximate speed and direction of the current. I made the pencil sextant to help me estimate my latitude. *Upper left:* The North Star, or Polaris, sits directly above the North Pole. (Magnetic north is another matter entirely.) One can see that the man standing on the pole of the globe to the lower left looks straight up at Polaris, an angle of 90 degrees to his horizontal, or horizon. The man on the equator sees the polestar right on his horizontal plane. The man in the raft at the upper right is looking at the polestar on the horizon, so he must be on the equator. The man on the globe who stands between the equator and the pole looks X degrees above his horizontal to see the polestar. He is then at X degrees of latitude, just like the man in the raft lower down. I lash together three pencils and set two of the arms at 18 degrees, which is my estimated latitude. I use the compass rose on the chart as a protractor, since it is conveniently divided up into 360 degrees. I must first line up the horizontal pencil with the horizon. Then, while trying not to move the instrument, I drop my eye so that I can look along the elevated pencil at Polaris. If Polaris is not in line, I adjust the angles of the pencils until it is, and then measure off my latitude from the compass rose. You can see on the chart that the islands bend off westward above 18 degrees and dramatically above 19. If I drift as high as 19 degrees, my voyage will last at least four days longer than at 18. If I go as high as 19.5 degrees, the voyage will lengthen by weeks, possibly months. My track is indicated by the broken line. The current flows in the direction of the arrow, trying to sweep me north. It will be very tight.

explain it rationally—perhaps that's the point. I don't think that these fish reflect or think as we do; their intelligence is of a different kind. While I cogitate about truth and meaning, they find them in their immediate and intense connection to life— in bodysurfing down huge waves, in chasing flying fish, in fighting for life on the end of my spear. I have often thought that my instincts were the tools that allowed me to survive so that my "higher functions" could continue. Now I am finding that it is more the other way around. It is my ability to reason that keeps command and allows me to survive, and the things I am surviving for are those that I want by instinct: life, companionship, comfort, play. The dorados have all of that here, now. How I wish I could become what I eat.

When I look down at my spear, I have more reason to wish I was a fish with no need for tools. It is broken again. I've been worried about the flimsy butter knife, but instead it's the stiff steel blade that has snapped cleanly off. I may be looking at my last supper. Now, don't be melodramatic; you've repaired it before. But what to use this time? The fork has already been used. My sheath knife is too bulky to drive through a dorado. There is nothing else from which to fashion a point. Well, I guess I'll just continue to use the butter knife. If it breaks, I'll try lashing on the sheath knife and go for triggers. I'll worry about it later.

Tainted canopy water, along with clear water caught in the space blanket, pours through the observation port drain when it rains. I push a piece of plastic tubing into a low point of drainage in the blanket and secure it with sail twine. A cloudburst at night sends water pouring in. I drain most of the foul water off on the kite and let the clean water drain from the tube into the Tupperware box. It's a gigantic success. I collect two and a half pints of water, still a bit tainted, but drinkable. If my last solar still blows completely, I'm not necessarily done for. I envision the dorado struggling for life on the end of my spear, twisting this way and that, this way and that. It brings to my mind the children's story of the little train trying ever so hard to puff up the mountain. I think I can, I think I can, I think I can . . . I know I can, I know I can, I know I can.

At noon I sight another ship headed north, too far away to see my flare. By now the flare gun is a frozen lump of rust anyway. The last meteor can't be fired. A handheld VHF radio might be a lot more effective than a flare gun. Many times at sea I have spoken to radio operators while my vessel has remained undetected by the eyes of the ship's crew. Well, no matter. Maybe the ship is a good sign. It's in a sensible position to be traveling from Brazil to the United States. Perhaps the lanes that I sketched in are correct. Inside this belt from Brazil to Florida, traffic will be heavier going to and from the Caribbean Islands, South America, and the U.S. Soon I should reach the continental shelf. Soon this will all end.

But the ocean remains endlessly the same—swimming pool blue, three miles deep, and thousands of miles across, the loneliest place on the planet. The movements of the fish are all reruns. The frigate birds hover overhead as if hung on strings from an immense mobile. I feel as if I am being filmed in an old Hollywood movie with a backdrop slowly moving past to give an illusion of motion.

I dream that I am home. Everything is calm and smells of spring. Light filters through budding leaves. Frisha, my ex-wife, and I sit on a stone wall. We wave to neighbors. I tell them all that I'm dying. They must send a search party for me.

My brother Ed and my father have collected as much information from the Coast Guard as they can. They've gotten reams of weather information from the Norfolk Weather Service. They send out letters to congressmen and congresswomen—to anyone who might conceivably help. Ed's fingers ache from whirling the telephone dial. His cigarette butts pile up until they send a landslide across the lip of the ashtray onto the table. My family examines the charts and the weather information to try and figure out where I most likely ran into trouble. Settling on the gale that began on February 3, they plot two probable drift patterns of my raft, using the two possible sailing routes that I would have taken. As a commercial diver and sailor, my brother knows the sea intimately. My father flew search-and-rescue missions in the war. Friends, professional sailors, sailmakers, and nautical journalists, many of whom have experienced disaster at sea, add their knowledge to the equation. My brother Bob and my mother keep the search furnace fired, make food, send letters, do the running. The results are remarkably accurate. One of the two positions they calculate is only one hundred miles from where I am.

The Coast Guard does not want to hear about any of this. A sailor this long overdue is certainly dead. Even should a search be reasonable, information gathered by a bunch of emotionally entangled amateurs could not possibly be equal to that of Coast Guard professionals.

Flurries of letters continue to pour forth from my parents' house. The yachting press keep their ears and phone lines open. Buddies of mine in Bermuda alert shipping across the Atlantic to be on the lookout, an effort the Guard refused to expend. Ham-radio operators spread the word about *Napoleon Solo* all over the lower North Atlantic.

But as each day passes, those who know the sea are increasingly aware of my slim chances for survival. Only one other man in all of history has survived this long alone at sea. Frisha has turned inward and buried her fears in her studies in plant science. My family is not yet aware that their energy will never result in a search, that at best their work keeps them occupied and their faith from being cast adrift. Those who still believe I'm out there alive are looked upon with increasing pity.

Oblivious to it all, I see only the same empty horizon that has spread out before me for two months. My limbs and eyelids are weighed down by fatigue. Even in the cool of day, when I must command myself to move for any reason, bitter arguments break out among the crew in my skull. Everything in the raft is saturated with salt, which draws moisture straight out of the air, even when conditions are relatively calm. This salty solution is smeared into every wound. Only at high noon does everything really dry out, and then the salt forms crusts that abrade my sores. The only position that is not agonizing is kneeling. Then,

APRIL 4
DAY 59

with the sun high overhead, I collapse in the intense heat. It would be so easy just to close my eyes and let go, so easy . . . Stop it! Get to work, I tell my scum-bucket crew. Work or she'll hang your hide for bird feed. Work, 'cause you ain't seen nothin' yet.

Using what's left of the stiff steel blade, I reinforce the flimsy butter knife on my lance. I pull the whole affair farther back on the shaft to stiffen it, but the shattered point appears too weak to withstand much strain. I will try a mild shock first. I jab at a trigger. I cannot drive the point through, but I am able to flick the poor fish aboard.

I am close now. I can feel it. I know how Columbus must have felt trying to keep his crew in order for each long day as they seemed to be sailing into oblivion, while he knew land was just over the horizon, always just over the horizon. The breasts of the birds overhead are dullish white, not red, but they must still be frigates. Two others have joined the ranks. Two terns flutter about. A gull-like brownish bird briefly flies across the water.

I have the nagging feeling that I am accompanied by someone. As I doze off, my companion assures me that he will keep watch or work on a project. Sometimes I remember conversations that have been shared, confidences, advice. I know it could not have happened, but the feeling persists. Fatigue is growing dangerous. My invisible companion assures me that I can last until April 20.

There is no fresh food left. The ocean is too rough for me to take good aim. Hard fish sticks soaked for several hours become soft enough to be chewable and salty enough to have some flavor. At first light, just before sunrise, I hold a piece of the hardtack in my mouth, the spear in my hand. Aim, strike, splash. Aim, strike, splash. I'm too slow, too weak. After hours of grueling patience, I have torn holes in five fish. The sun rises. My arms tremble and seem to melt. I collapse on the wet floor of my raft. Failed. Again in the evening. Failed. Again in the morning. Failed.

In these temperatures, survival time without water is as short as three days. Do I have ten days' strength? I try to tend the still. Another fish bites through the distillate collection bag, draining more fresh water back into the sea. I sit calmly downcast.

For days the Atlantic has been barren, but now I see a huge clump of sargasso weed riding the waves. As it comes nearer, I dog paddle over and pull the weed onto *Ducky*'s

APRIL 6
DAY 61

bib. There are things crawling and fishing line tangled in it. Another bundle bobs up ahead. I throw the first onto *Ducky*'s stern and grab the second, then a third, and a fourth. The ocean begins to get thick with the weed. I hurry to pick through the layers of vegetation, finding an abundance of the usual fare of flexing shrimp, flipping fish, and clicking crabs. I throw the sargasso onto the back of the raft for later and grab the next clump. A black crust appears on the horizon ahead.

We drift through a line of weed piled up like autumn leaves. The sargasso is laced with trash. For sixty days the ocean has been pristine, a world that might never have been touched by man. Ships and a single chunk of Styrofoam have been the only evidence that humans still inhabit the earth. Suddenly my surroundings are full of their excrement—*our* excrement, I remind myself. Old bottles, baskets, clotted clumps of oil, bobbing bulbs, flasks, fishnet webs, ropes, crates, floats, foam, and faded fabric. The highway of trash stretches from south to north as far as I can see. For hours *Ducky* wades through one lane of rubbish after another. The highway is miles wide.

The triggers go crazy and dart off this way and that, pecking at the various bits of life trapped within the waste. In a strange way, I feel revived, at ease, untroubled. The sea thrives on the garbage. Crabs and barnacles abound. Nature's nurseries lie in the most unlikely lands. To us decay is death, but to Nature it is another beginning.

I fill my mouth with the crabs and shrimp that have been

squirreled away within this oceanic dump. It seems ironic that this pollution should serve as a signpost of my salvation. I'm on the oily brick road to Oz, and food, shelter, and clothing are just off at the next exit. The new birds and fish that I have been seeing are signs that I've made significant progress. And this road of trash is a major demarcation of some kind, a billboard that indicates major upwelings or changes of current.

Night falls as *Ducky* and I continue to drift through the pollution. In the morning the water is lighter blue and sparkling clear. I'm convinced that I have reached the shallower waters of the continental shelf. My destiny lies directly ahead.

THE
DUTCHMAN

T HE SEA RUNS BY in its usual form, five-foot, maybe six-foot rollers ribboning westward. The wind is a steady twenty to twenty-five knots—lively but not dangerous.

Rubber Ducky rises to each surge and softly falls again. I stand, wobbling, my brain stuffed with images of food and drowned by dreams of drink. They are all I can think about, that and the rolling waves that snap around me. I divide the horizon into six segments. I scan one segment while balancing as best I can. Then I carefully turn, get reacclimated, and scan the next. When it's stormy, I often have to await an ascent to a large peak before I can see very far, but in these conditions nearly every wave top will do. A ship squats, five to eight miles off. She's heading west northwest; might come a little closer. I await the right moment and pull the pin. My last parachute flare pops, sizzles skyward, and bursts. It is not as bright as it would be at night, looks more like a star poking its head through the murky sky. Ship number seven shyly slinks away. Only three flares are left, all handheld. A ship will have to run me down before it sees me now. Reaching the islands is my only hope.

Hesitantly I chance the final destruction of my spear and manage to impale another dorado. Mechanically I cut it up, slice the thick fillets into strips, poke holes in the strips, and hang them. It seems barbaric. I don't want to kill any more. Please let me land soon. When I am gone, how will my fish feel? How will I feel without them?

Now that I have fresh fish, I won't have to work as hard for the next couple of days. It's a moment's respite, though I know that I will never be able to rest until the voyage ends. It's almost unbelievable to think of how much time I had to spare in *the old days*, back before my equipment was failing regularly and before I became half starved. Now each job takes longer and longer to accomplish. I continually wonder how much more a body can take. I don't consider suicide—not now, after all I have come through—but I can understand how others might see it as a reasonable option in these circumstances. For me it is always easier to struggle on. To give myself courage, I tell myself that my hell could be worse, that it might get worse and I must prepare for that. My body is certain to deteriorate further. I tell myself that I can handle it. Compared to what others have been through, I'm fortunate. I tell myself these things over and over, building up fortitude, but parts of my body feel as if they are in flames. The fire from the sores on my back, butt, and legs shrieks upward and the flames burst forth into my skull. In a moment my spirit is in ashes and tears well in my eyes. They are not enough to even dampen the conflagration.

Kneeling in front of the doorway, I can raise my wounds from the salty cushions. The sun beats down on my head, and I slump across the bow. Dorados are drawn to my protruding knees and wheel around the raft all day long. They know I am not hunting. The triggers too seem to know when I have my spear in hand. I drag my arm through the cool water, as clear as glass. As the dorados slither out from under me, our eyes are only a foot apart. I sweep my hand toward them. I have never seen them touch one another, though I suppose they sometimes do, yet they let me stroke their slippery bodies. As soon as my fingers touch down, the dorados flip away as if irritated, but they return time and again. They have me trained, you see— successful wildlife management. How easy it would be to let go and die, to undergo the transformation into other bits of the universe, to be eaten by fish, to become fish. A dorado slips out and I graze the feathery flip of her tail. The little flirt immediately returns. But I can't let go. People are my tribe. It should be easy to surrender to the dorados or the sea, but it is not.

I measure my latitude with my sextant. About eighteen degrees. How accurate is it? I know now I will never last another twenty days. If I am too far north, I am done for. If I could manage the wind, I would make it take me south.

In the morning the dorados are gone. Several of a new type of triggerfish appear. They are almost black, with bright blue spots, puckered mouths, and fins like chiffon collars rolling in a breeze. They look to me like oceanic starlets. I call them my little coquettes.

APRIL 10
DAY 65

Two long fish torpedo under the raft. They are even faster than the old blue dorados, though they must be a type of dorado. They're smaller than the blue dorados—two and a half to three feet—and their skin is a mottled green and brown, like army camouflage. One of them looks badly damaged: raw, pink skin shows where most of the camouflage has fallen away in large sheaths. I think of it as having ichthyofaunic mange.

Tiny black fish, maybe an inch or two long, sweep along before the raft, contrasting sharply with the Atlantic's topaz blue. Their bodies wiggle as if made of soft rubber. *Ducky*'s slow forward progress creates small ripples, what could jokingly be called a bow wave. Just as porpoises ride the pressure waves that are created by a ship's bow rushing through the sea, so these tiny black fish swab little arcs just ahead of *Ducky*'s backwash. I try to scoop them up with my coffee can, but they are always too fast.

Since the long battle to repair *Ducky*'s bottom tube, I've been pretty wiped out, but I feel a little stronger this evening. For the first time in over a week, I return to my yoga routine, first spreading out my cushion and sleeping bag to cushion the dorados' blows. The hemorrhoids are puffed out again, and my hollow butt provides little protection. I sit up, bend one scrawny leg until my heel rests firmly in my crotch, and then touch my head to the knee of my straightened leg, while grasping the foot of that leg with both hands. I perfect a twisting exercise while hanging on to the handline. Then I lie on my stomach and lift my head as if doing a pushup, but I keep my legs and hips on the floor and bend my spine back into a wheel. I scoot forward, lie on my back, raise my legs over my head, and bring them around until my feet hit the floor behind me. My body weaves about like a stock of kelp swaying in the currents. I have not only sea legs but sea arms and a sea back, perhaps even a sea brain.

My head is struck hard. I wiggle my jaw to see if it is loose. The new camouflaged dorados are very powerful and aggressive. They bombard the raft all day long, ramming it with their bullet heads, slapping at it with their bullwhip tails, and blasting off with incredible speed. I leap to the entrance and grab the spear, but they are always long gone. Sometimes I glimpse their tails as they shoot off into the distance. Sometimes I see them racing by, several fathoms below. They never move calmly like the big blue dorados. They always move frantically, like they're hopped up on speed.

As the sun sets, I hear squeaking again and spy some big black porpoises, purposefully cutting their way to the west. They do not come close, but I feel touched by the graceful ease with which they glide through the Atlantic's swell.

The frigate birds, three of them now, are still frozen in position, riding the invisible waves of the sky high above the water. I'm impressed that their delicate long wings survive the power of the sea. They are often above me at first light, or they drift up from the west soon after. Another snowy tern shows up; it is unbelievable that this tiny bird migrates eleven thousand miles every year.

A dark gray bird swings back and forth, approaching from where the clouds go, slowly getting closer. It flies like a crow. I tell myself that it must come from land. More important, it is a flying lump of food. It nears. I duck behind the canopy. I can't see it, but I hear it fluttering at the entrance to my cave, contemplating entry. It flaps away. I wait. A shadow flickers on the canopy, grows, and a slight weight puts an imprint on the tent peak. Cautiously I bend forward and see the bird perched,

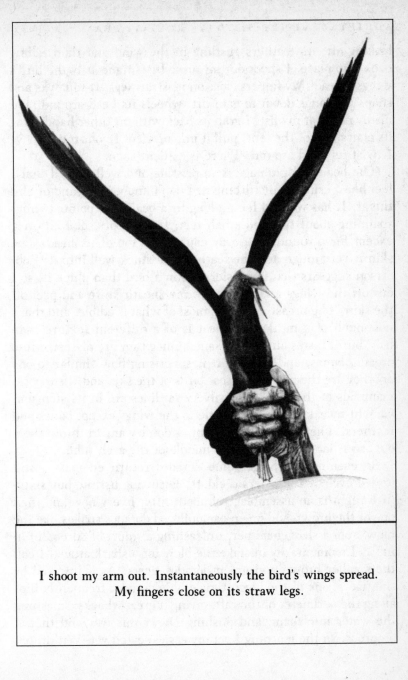

I shoot my arm out. Instantaneously the bird's wings spread.
My fingers close on its straw legs.

looking aft, its feathers rustling in the wind and then falling back into place. I shoot out my arm. Instantaneously the bird's wings spread. My fingers close on its straw legs. It squawks and snaps its wings down to gain lift, wheels its head around, and madly pecks at my fist. I grab its back with my other hand, drag its claws free of the tent, pull it into my den. In one quick move I twist its head around. There is a silent snap.

The beautiful plumage is so pristine and well tended that I feel like a criminal disturbing it. I don't know what kind of bird this is. It has webbed feet, a long thin beak, and pointed wings spanning about two and a half feet. It is a sooty color all over, except for a round light gray cap on the top of its head. The skin is very tough and the feathers are stuck well into it. Robertson suggests that it's easier to skin a bird than pluck it, so I cut off the wings and head with my sheath knife and peel off the skin. The breast makes up most of what is edible, and that's not much of a meal. The meat is of a different texture than fish, but it tastes almost the same. Once they are dissected into organs, bones, and muscle, it is surprising how similar to one another are the fish of the sea, birds of the sky, and, I suppose, mammals of the land. Five silvery sardines are in its stomach. Caught near land? There's little to the wings except bones and feathers. They're quite beautiful. I don't want to throw them out, so I hang them from the middle of the arch tube.

By evening the bigger blue dorados return en masse, still lorded over by the emerald elders. Escorting us into our sixty-fifth night is an assemblage of about fifty. Every now and then one of the brown and green camouflaged dorados strikes like the blow from a sledgehammer, unleashing a squirt of adrenalin in me as I momentarily mistake the blow for a shark attack. I call the smaller brown and green dorados tigers. As if inspired by the tigers, one of the biggest male blue dorados frequently flips along the perimeter of the raft, giving it great whacks, smashing the water into foam, and pushing *Ducky* this way and that. I ignore it. In the morning I get my easiest catch yet. Within ten minutes and using only two shots, I have a fine female hauled aboard.

By nightfall the waves have reared up again and ricochet off of *Ducky*'s stern. Each wave that breaks on the raft echoes through the tubes and sounds like a blast from a shotgun going off next to my ear. The wind catches the water catchment cape, snaps it up and down, rips its buttonholes wider, and tries to tear it away. During the night conditions become wilder. Watery fists knock *Ducky* back and forth. I huddle athwartships, getting as far forward as I dare in an effort to stay dry while also trying to keep the stern down. Although the front of the canopy gives a little better protection, dryness is still relative. The back of the canopy is little more than a stretched rag. Wave crests fall on it and drain through onto my face, stinging my eyes and pouring into my sleeping bag. I continually wipe the water off the floor and the canopy, but everything is soaked in no time.

It is April 12, the date that marked the anniversary of my marriage such a very long time ago. Frisha's life as my wife was not easy. I'd take off on a delivery trip or a passage and leave her behind. Some- APRIL 12 times we wouldn't see each other for months. DAY 67 She thought that it was all a very risky business, despite my reassurances. Not long before I left the States on *Solo*, she told me that she thought I would eventually meet my maker at sea, but that it would not be during this voyage. I wonder how she feels about it now. I wonder if she was right. What is Frisha doing? She must believe that I am dead while she studies to bring life from the soil. One day, perhaps, long after I am drowned and consumed by fish, a fisherman may haul aboard a catch that will find its way to her table. She will take the head, tail, and bones and heap them upon her compost pile, mix them with the soil so green life will sprout. Nature knows no waste.

A flying fish crashes onto the canopy behind the solar still. I am losing my taste for fish, but any change from dorado arouses my appetite. My guts feel like they have fallen right out of me. No amount of fish can fill my vacant stomach. I sit up, grab the flyer, and wonder if it is scared or if it accepts death like another swimming stroke.

Maintaining discipline becomes more difficult each day. My fearsome and fearful crew mutter mutinous misgivings within the fo'c's'le of my head. Their spokesman yells at me.

"Water, Captain! We need more water. Would you have us die here, so close to port? What is a pint or two? We'll soon be in port. We can surely spare a pint—"

"Shut up!" I order. "We don't know how close we are. Might have to last to the Bahamas. Now, get back to work."

"But, Captain—"

"You heard me. You've got to stay on ration."

They gather together, mumbling among themselves, greedily eyeing the bags of water dangling from *Ducky*'s bulwarks. We are shabby, almost done for. Legs already collapsed. Torso barely holds head up. Empty as a tin drum. Only arms have any strength left. It is indeed pitiful. Perhaps the loss of a pint would not hurt. No, I must maintain order. "Back to work," I say. "You can make it."

Yet I feel swayed more and more by my body's demands, feel stretched so tight between my body, mind, and spirit that I might snap at any moment. The solar still has another hole in it, and the distillate is more often polluted with salt water. I can detect less and less often when it is reasonably unsalty. I may go mad at any time. Mutiny will mean the end. I know I am close to land. I must be. I must convince us all.

We've been over the continental shelf for four days. One of my small charts shows the shelf about 120 miles to the east of the West Indies. I should see the tall, green slopes of an island, if my sextant is correct. I should hit Antigua—ironically, my original destination. But who knows? I could be hundreds of miles off. This triangle of pencils may be a foolish bit of junk. The chart could be grossly inaccurate. I spend endless hours scanning the horizon for a cloud shape that does not move, searching the sky for a long wisp of cloud that might suggest human flight. Nothing. I feel like a watch slowly winding down, a Timex thrown out of an airplane just once too often. I've overestimated my speed, or perhaps I'm drifting diagonally across the shelf. If there was only some way to measure the current. I'm assuming that I'm within two hundred miles of my calculated position, but if I've been off by as little as five miles a day, I could be four hundred miles away from where I hope I am— another eight or even fifteen days. "Water, Captain. Please? Water." Tick, tick, slower and slower. When will it stop? Can I wind it up until the end of the month without breaking the spring?

The next afternoon's sun is scorching. The solar still keeps passing out and looks as if it may not last much longer. By mid– bake-off I can feel myself begin to panic and shiver.

"More water, Captain. We must have more."

"No! No! Well, maybe. No! You can't have any. Not a drop."

The heat pours down. My flesh feels as if it is turning to desert sand. I cannot sit upright without having trouble focusing. Everything is foggy.

"Please, Captain. Water. Now, before it's too late."

O.K. The tainted water. You can drink as much of it as you want. But the clear water remains. One pint of it a day. That's the limit. It's the limit until we see aircraft or land. Agreed?"

I hesitate. "Yes, all right."

A sludge of orange particles sits in the bottom of the plastic tube in which the wretched canopy water rests. I triple layer my T-shirt and strain the water through it into a tin again and again. The result is a pint of cloudy liquid. It is bitter. I can just keep it down.

My thirst becomes stronger. Within an hour I must drink more. In another hour more still. Soon the bitter pint is gone. It is as if my whole body has turned to ash. I must drink even more.

"No. Can't. No more until tomorrow."

"But we must. You've poisoned us now and we must."

"Stop it!" I must keep command. But my eyes are wild, my limbs shaking in an effort to hold back the panic.

My torso screams out. "Take it!" Limbs reach out for a sack of water

"No!" I scramble to my knees, almost in tears. I get to my feet and look aft for a moment. I can't stand forever but for now the breeze cools me off.

There, in the sky—a jet! Not just a contrail or the faintest hint of a jet, but a silver-bodied bird streaking to Brazil! Quick, man, the EPIRB! Battery is probably shot. Well, the light's on at least and he can't be more than ten miles away. I'll leave it on for twelve hours. The jet looks small. It may not be a commercial flight. Regardless, it couldn't have come at a better time. We must be close. I fulfill my promise. I hand out a pint of clean, sweet water. Everybody relaxes.

A gooselike bird resembling a gannet flies over. It has even-colored brown plumage, except for dark rings around its eyes. Yesterday a jaeger winged by. It was not supposed to be there. Should I inform these birds that they are beyond their prescribed ranges? New fish, new birds, different water color, no sargasso. It all adds up. This voyage *will* end soon. I stare intensely at the horizon until my eyes water.

The Miami Coast Guard is contacted by a ship off Puerto Rico that has sighted a small white boat, dismasted and adrift. The Coast Guard requests that the ship board the vessel. Negative. The boat is already lost to sight. The ship will not return. Description? White, twenty feet long, no markings, no one on board.

Solo was beige. She had a wide dark blue stripe all around the topsides and dark blue cabin sides. Her name was painted across her transom. A fourteen-inch-high number 57 was plastered on each side and on her deck.

Somehow the two boats are taken to be the same. Officially, "*Napoleon Solo* has been located with no one on board." In

California, a ham operator picks up the message from the Long Beach Coast Guard and begins to notify those who have been keeping their ears open. Messages flock out. *Solo* is no longer missing.

My brother demands more information. Was the life raft on board? Was any other equipment visible? Were there any signs of possible piracy? What was the wreck's position? He wants to go check it out himself. The New York Coast Guard knows nothing of the matter. It proves impossible to get any information at all from them. Something funny seems to be going on. While my arm trails through the water stroking my doggies, my mother envisions me murdered by pirates or rotting in some fascist prison cell.

Indeed, something funny is going on. The Coast Guard begins to issue statements. At first they say that the message that *Solo* has been located must be a bogus one made by a ham operator without a license. Then they hint that it may have been sent by the Callahans themselves in order to stir up some action.

Slowly and meticulously, my family trace the message through the ham net to Germany and then to California, and then from Long Beach to Miami through the holes in the Coast Guard net. The truth has escaped. Still, the false message is being carried on the seafarer's net and is received by a friend of mine in Bermuda. The New York Coast Guard instructs the Callahans that if they want the message canceled, they will have to arrange it themselves. Finally it is done.

By this time my family have done everything they can to calculate my approximate position and get a search going. They have tried in vain to get the armed forces to fly over the areas of high probability during their routine patrols and maneuvers. They have also failed in attempts to gain the use of spy satellites that have the acuity to photograph trash cans from space. Not only is the target not specific in this case, but the area to be searched is at least 200 miles across, or 31,400 square miles. If each photo covered 900 square feet, or 30 feet on a side, it would take over a billion photos to check out the area. In every direction in which my family have turned to get a physical search under way, they have found a roadblock.

There is little else for them to do but to continue writing to politicians and maintain private contact with shipping companies. Although most people now feel I must have perished long ago, my parents decide that only if I don't show in six months will they consider the matter laid to rest. My brother Ed readies himself to return to his family in Hawaii. It is now just a waiting game for us all.

Finally, on April 20, the Coast Guard decides to rebroadcast for another week the message that *Solo* is overdue.

The past few days have passed ever so slowly and I have been growing progressively more dim and depressed. We should have reached the islands days ago. We couldn't have passed between them, could we? No, they are too close together. I'd have seen at least one.

APRIL 16

DAY 71

And the birds still come at me from the west. When do I use the EPIRB for the last time? Even with the short range it must now have, the massive daytime Caribbean air traffic will hear the signal. But I must wait until I see land or can last no longer.

I am beginning to doubt everything—my position, my senses, my life itself. Maybe I am Prometheus, cursed to have my liver torn out each day and have it grow back each night. Maybe I am the Flying Dutchman, doomed to sail the seas forever and never rest again, to watch my own body rot and my equipment deteriorate. I am in an infinite vortex of horror, whirling deeper and deeper. Thinking of what I will do when it is all over is a bad joke. It will never be over. It is worse than death. If I were to search the most heinous parts of my mind to create a vision of a real hell, this would be the scene, exactly.

The last solar still has completely blown, just like the one before. The bottom cloth has rotted and ripped away. I have a full stock of water, but it will go quickly. Rainfall is my only well now.

I continue to take note of the positive signs of approaching landfall. The tiger dorados have gone. A five- or ten-pound mottled brown fish, a tripletail, has lumbered around *Rubber Ducky* for two days. I've tried to hit it, but I've been impatient. I hurried the shots and only managed to poke it twice, driving it away. There have been more sooty birds in the sky, and the frigates continue to reel about overhead. I've grabbed two snowy terns, which landed for a short rest and received a permanent sleep. I've seen another ship, but at night and very far off. Somehow all of these changes do little for my continued depression. I am the Dutchman. I arise still feeling asleep. There is no time for relaxation, only time for stress. Work harder. Do more. Must it last forever?

APRIL 18

DAY 73

I strike my fishing pose yet again. My aching arms grasp the few ounces of plastic and aluminum, the butter knife tied on like a caveman's stone point, but indubitably less effective. Now I can hold the pose only for a minute or so, no longer. The dorados brush against my knees as I push all of my weight down on one knee, then the other. They turn their sides to me as if wanting to show off the target area, and they swing out to the left and right or flip around deep below. Occasionally they wiggle their heads so near the surface that the water welters up. Perhaps one will rise and speak to me like the flounder in the fairy tale. Often I wait a microsecond too long, and the few square inches of bull's eye melt away into the dark water, which is just starting to brighten as the sun rises. This time I strike home, the battle rages, and I win again. The emerald elders court behind the lines like generals who are smart enough not to join in the melee any more.

Clouds race across my world, gray and smeared, too light for a heavy burst of rain, but the light sprinkles and misty air, combined with wave spray stirred up by the wind, prevent my fish from drying properly. Temporarily though, the stock of food allows me to concentrate my energy on designing new water-catchment systems. The first is simple. I stretch plastic from the cut-up still along the shaft of the spear gun. I can hold it out, away from the sheltering canopy, pulling a corner with my mouth. Next I set the blown still on the bow. I punch it into a flat, round plate and curl up the edges like a deep-dish pizza pie. Even in light showers, I can see that the two devices work. A fine mist collects into drops, that streak into dribbles, that run into wrinkled, plastic valleys, where I can slurp them up. I must move quickly to tend to each system and collect water before it's polluted by waves or the canopy. I am far enough west that the clouds are beginning to collect, and occasionally I see a "black cow," as some sailors call squally cumulus, grazing far off, its rain streaking to earth.

I stick with the routine that I've followed for two and a half months. At night I take a look around each time I awaken. Every half hour during the day, I stand and carefully peruse the horizon in all directions. I have done this more than two thousand times now. Instinctively I know how the waves roll, when one will duck and weave to give a clear view for another hundred yards or half a mile. This noon a freighter streams up from astern, a bit to the north of us. The hand flares are nearly invisible in the daylight, so I choose an orange smoke flare and pop it. The dense orange genie spreads its arms out and flies off downwind just above the water. Within a hundred feet it has been blown into a haze thinner than the smoke of a crowded pub. The ship cuts up the Atlantic a couple of miles abeam and smoothly steams off to the west. She *must* be headed to an island port.

I work all the rest of the day and all of the morning of April 19 to create an elaborate water collection device. Using the aluminum tubing from the radar reflector and my last dead solar still, I make *Rubber Ducky* a bonnet that I secure to the summit of the canopy arch tube. The half circle of aluminum tubing keeps the face of the bonnet open and facing aft. A bridle adjusts the angle of the face, which I keep nearly vertical, and the wind

APRIL 19
DAY 74

blows the bonnet forward like a bag. I fit a drain and tubing that I can run inside to fill up containers while I tend to the other water collectors.

For hours I watch white, fluffy cumulus rise up from the horizon and slowly pass. Sometimes they band together and form dense herds running in long lines. Those that have grazed over the Atlantic long enough grow thick and muscular, rearing up to great billowing heights, churning violently, their underbellies flat and black. When they can hold no more, their rain thunders down in black streaks that lash the sea. I chew upon dried sticks of dorado awaiting the test of my new tools.

But it seems that the paths of the squalls are bound to differ from mine. Sometimes a long line of clouds passes close by. I watch the wispy edges swirl above me and feel a few drops or a momentary sprinkle coming down. It's just enough to show me that my new water collection gear is very effective. I'm convinced that I'll collect several pints, maybe even a gallon, if I can just get directly in the path of a single heavy shower. It's one thing to have a tool and quite another to be in a position to use it. My eyes wander from the horizon to the sky. I'm so tired of always awaiting something.

Seventy-five days—April 20. With the drizzle and the salt spray, my dorado sticks have grown pasty rather than drying. I'm astonished that the dried sticks from one of the first dorados that I caught still seem to be fine. Only a slight whitish haze covers the deep amber, woody interior.

For an hour in late afternoon, I watch a drove of clouds run up from the east. I can tell that they're traveling a little to the south of my course. As they rise up and charge onward, I ready myself, swallowing frequently, though there is no saliva to swallow. I try to wish them into running me down, but they ignore me and begin to sweep by about a mile away, clattering and flashing with lightning. Four separate heavy columns of rain pour down, so dense that they eclipse the blue sky behind. I watch tons of pure water flowing down like aerial waterfalls. If

APRIL 20

DAY 75

Using the aluminum tubing from the radar reflector and the plastic from the last dead solar still, I create an elaborate water collection device—a bonnet that sits on the peak of the arch tube. I bend and lash together the aluminum tubing into a semicircle with an axle that runs across the bottom. All of the ends are well padded to prevent damage to the raft's canopy or arch tube. This framework keeps the face of the bonnet open and facing the wind. The plastic still is lashed to the framework and blows forward like a small sail. I've fitted a piece of tubing into the bottom of the bonnet and led it inside so that when it rains I can keep busy filling containers. The bridle tied to the stern keeps the bonnet upright, but I can adjust the angle so that the face can point directly into the rain. Also note that the water collection cape is beginning to deteriorate and tear. I've pulled up the rusty gas bottle and have it tied to the exterior handline. For hours each day I stand and keep watch, often gazing ahead, hoping for the cloud formations to finally reveal land.

only I could be just a mile from where I am. No sips, no single mouthfuls, but an overflow of water I could guzzle. If only *Ducky* could sail instead of waddle. I have missed. My collection devices are bone dry and flutter in the wind.

~~~~~~~~~~~~DEATH

of my seventy-fifth day are smudged with clouds migrating westward. A drizzle falls, barely more than a fog, but any amount
of saltless moisture causes me to jump into action. For two hours
I swing my plastic buckets through the air, collecting a pint and
a half. My catchment systems *will* do the trick.

As long as the waves are not too large, I do not worry about
capsizing, so I curl up and sleep against the bow. These days
it takes so long to choke out the pain and fall asleep. When I
do, it is only an hour or less before a sharp stab from a wound
or sore awakens me.

I arise to survey the black waters, which occasionally flash
with phosphorescent lines from a breaking wave or the flight of
a fish. A soft glow looms just to the south of dead ahead. And
there, just to the north, is another. A fishing fleet? They do not
move. My God, these are no ships! It is the nighttime halo of
land that I detect! Standing, I glimpse a flip of light from the
side. A lighthouse beam, just over the horizon, sweeps a wide
bar of light like a club beating out a rhythm—flash, pause,
flash-flash, rest; flash, pause, flash-flash. It *is* land. "Land!" I
shout. "Land ho!" I'm dancing up and down, flinging my arms
about, as if hugging an invisible companion. I can't believe it!

This calls for a real celebration! Break out the drinks! In big,
healthy swallows, I down two pints. I swagger and feel as light-
headed as if it were pure alcohol. I look out time and again to
confirm that this is no illusion. I pinch myself. Ouch! Yes, and
I have gotten the water to my lips and down my throat, which
I've never been able to do in a dream. No, it isn't any dream.
Oh real, how real! I bounce about like an idiot. I'm having quite
a time.

O.K., now, calm down. You aren't home yet. What lighthouse
is that? Antigua doesn't make sense. Are you north or south?

Ducky is aimed down the empty corridor between the two glows that I see. When I get closer maybe I can paddle some, or maybe I can strap the paddles onto *Ducky*'s tubes to act like center-boards. Even if I can't hit land, the EPIRB will surely bring help. When the sun rises I'll flick the switch one last time.

I can hardly sleep but manage to drop off for a half hour now and again. Each time I awaken, I look out to confirm that this isn't the ultimate elaborate dream. Another glow begins to emerge dead ahead. Morning, I hope, will reveal the rim of an island down low on the horizon, close enough to reach before nightfall. A landing in daylight will be dangerous enough. If I reach the island tomorrow night . . . Well, one thing at a time. Rest now.

Dawn of the seventy-sixth day arrives. I can't believe the rich panorama that meets my eyes. It is full of green. After months of little other than blue sky, blue fish, and blue sea, the brilliant, verdant green is overwhelming. It is not just the rim of one island that is ahead, as I had expected. To the south a mountainous island as lush as Eden juts out of the sea and reaches up toward the clouds. To the north is another island with a high peak. Directly ahead is a flat-topped isle — no vague outline, but in full living color. I'm five to ten miles out and headed right for the center. The northern half is composed of vertical cliffs against which the Atlantic smashes to foam. To the south the land slopes down to a long beach above which a few white buildings perch, probably houses.

APRIL 21

DAY 76

Close as I am, I'm not safe yet. A landing is bound to be treacherous. If I hit the northern shore, I run the risk of being crushed against the sharp coral cliffs. To the south I'll have to rake across wide reefs before I hit the beach. Even if I get that far without being ripped to ribbons, I doubt I'll be able to walk or even crawl to get help. One way or the other, this voyage will end today, probably by late afternoon.

I flip on the EPIRB, and for the first time I break out the medical kit. As with all of my supplies, I have been saving it until I absolutely needed it. I take out some cream, smear it all

over my sores, and fashion a diaper from the triangular bandage.
I'll try to coerce *Ducky* to sail around the south side of the island,
so I don't have to land through the breakers on the windward
side. If *Ducky* refuses, I'll go for the beach. I'll need all the
protection I can get. I'll wrap the foam cushion around my torso,
which will keep me afloat and serve as a buffer against the coral.
I'll cut off *Rubber Ducky*'s canopy, so that I won't get trapped
inside and so I can wrap my legs and arms with the fabric.

I'll try to keep *Ducky* upright and ride her in, though the
bottom tube will certainly be torn to bits. Everything must be
orderly and secure. I rummage around, throwing out pieces of
junk that I won't need and making room in my bags for the first
aid kit and the other necessities. I gnaw on a couple of fish
sticks, but they taste like lumps of tallow. I can survive with
no more food. My doggies nudge at me. Yes, my friends, I will
soon leave you. On what separate paths will we travel? I pitch
the remaining rancid fish sticks and save only a few of the dried
amber ones as souvenirs. Ah, yes, another pint of water to fortify
myself for the landing.

As each wave passes, I hear something new. RRrrr . . .
RRrrr . . . It grows louder. An engine! I leap to my knees.
Coming from the island, a couple of hundred yards away, a
sharp white bow, flared out at the rail, pitches forward against
a wave and then crashes down with a splash. The boat climbs
and falls, getting closer and closer. It's small, maybe twenty
feet, and is made of roughhewn wood painted white, with a
green stripe around the gunwale. Three incredulous dark faces
peer toward me. Jumping to my feet, I wave to them and yell,
"Hello!" They wave back. This time I have definitely been seen.
I am saved! I can't believe it, just can't believe . . . Nearly over.
No reef crossing, no anxious awaiting of an airplane. Two of
the men are golden mahogany in color, and the third is black.
The one at the helm wears a floppy straw hat with a wide brim
that flaps up and down. His T-shirt flags out behind him as he
rounds his boat ahead of me and slides to a halt. The three of
them are about my age and seem perplexed as they loudly babble

to one another in a strange tongue. It's been almost three months since I've heard another human voice.

"*Hablar español?*" I yell.

"No, no!" What is it that they say?

"*Parlez-vous français?*" I can't make out their reply. They all talk at the same time. I motion to the islands. "What islands?"

"Aahh." They seem to get it. "Guadeloupe, Guadeloupe." French. But it sure isn't like any French I've ever heard. It's Creole, I learn later, a rapid-fire, pidgin French. In a few minutes I figure out that the blackest of them is speaking English, with a Calypso beat and heavy Caribbean accent. I'd probably have trouble comprehending another New Englander at this point, but I begin to put it all together.

We sit in our tiny boats, rising and falling on the waves, only yards apart. For several moments we stop talking and stare at one another, not knowing quite what to say. Finally they ask me, "Whatch you doing, man? Whatch you want?"

"I'm on the sea for seventy-six days." They turn to each other, chattering away loudly. Perhaps they think I embarked from Europe in *Rubber Ducky III* as a stunt. "Do you have any fruit?" I ask.

"No, we have nothing like that with us." As if confused and not knowing what they should do, the ebony one asks instead, "You want to go to the island now?"

Yes, oh, definitely yes, I think, but I say nothing immediately. Their boat rolls toward me and then away, empty of fish. The present, the past, and the immediate future suddenly seem to fit together in some inexplicable way. I know that my struggle is over. The door to my escape has been fortuitously flung open by these fishermen. They are offering me the greatest gift possible: life itself. I feel as if I have struggled with a most demanding puzzle, and after fumbling for the key piece for a long time, it has fallen into my fingers. For the first time in two and a half months, my feelings, body, and mind are of one piece.

The frigates hover high above, drawn to me by my dorados and the flying fish on which they both feed. These fishermen

saw the birds, knew there were fish here, and came to find
them. They found me; but not me *instead* of their fish, me *and*
their fish. Dorados. They have sustained me and have been my
friends. They nearly killed me, too, and now they are my salvation. I am delivered to the hands of fishermen, my brothers
of the sea. They rely on her just as I have. Their hooks, barbs,
and bludgeons are similar to my own. Their clothing is as simple.
Perhaps their lives are as poor. The puzzle is nearly finished.
It is time to fit the last piece.

"No, I'm O.K. I have plenty of water. I can wait. You fish.
Fish!" I yell as if reaching a revelation. "Plenty of fish, big fish,
best fish in the sea!" They look at each other, talking. I urge
them. "Plenty of fish here, you *must* fish!"

One bends over the engine and gives the line a yank. The
boat leaps forward. They bait six-inch hooks with silvery fish
that look like flyers without big wings. Several lines are tossed
overboard, and in a moment, amidst tangled Creole yells and
flailing arms, the engine is cut. One of them gives a heave, and
a huge dorado jumps through the air in a wide arc and lands
with a thud in the bottom of the boat. They roar off again, and
before they've gone two hundred yards they stop and yank two
more fat fish aboard. Their yelling never stops. Their caco-
phonous Creole becomes more jumbled and wild, as if short-
circuiting from the overload of energy in the fishing frenzy.
Repeatedly they open the throttle and the boat leaps forward.
They bail frantically, cast out hooks, give their lines a jerk, and
stop. The stern wave rushes up, lifts and pats the boat's rear.
More fish are hauled from the sea.

I calmly open my water tins. Five pints of my hoarded wealth
flow down my throat. I watch the dorados below me, calmly
swimming about. Yes, we part here, my friends. You do not
seem betrayed. Perhaps you do not mind enriching these poor
men. They will never again see a catch the likes of you. What
secrets do you know that I cannot even guess?

I wonder why I chanced to pack my spear gun in my emergency bag, why *Solo* stayed afloat just long enough for me to get

my equipment. Why, when I had trouble hunting, did the dorado come closer? Why did they make it increasingly easier for me as I and my weapon became more broken and weak, until in the end they lay on their sides right under my point? Why have they provided me just enough food to hang on for eighteen hundred nautical miles? I know that they are only fish, and I am only a man. We do what we must and only what Nature allows us to do in this life. Yet sometimes the fabric of life is woven into such a fantastic pattern. I needed a miracle and my fish gave it to me. That and more. They've shown me that miracles swim and fly and walk, rain down and roll away all around me. I look around at life's magnificent arena. The dorados seem almost to be leaping into the fishermen's arms. I have never felt so humble, nor so peaceful, free, and at ease.

Tiny letters on the boat's quarters spell out her name, *Clemence*. She roars off one way and then the other, circling around *Rubber Ducky*, around and around. The men are pulling in a fish a minute. They swing by every so often to see if I'm all right. I wave to them. They come very close, and one of them holds out a bundle of brown paper as *Clemence* glides by. I unwrap the gift and behold a great prize: a mound of chipped coconut cemented together with raw brown sugar and capped with a dot of red sugar. Red! Even simple colors take on a miraculous significance.

"Coco sucré," one yells as they roar off again to continue the hunt. My smile—God, it's so strange to smile—feels wrapped right around my head. Sugar and fruit at the same time. I peel off a shard of coconut and lay it upon my watering tongue. I carefully chip away at the *coco sucré* like a sculptor working on a piece of granite, but I eat it all, every last bit of it.

Slowly the dorados below thin out. The fishermen are slowing down. A doggie comes by every so often as if to say farewell before shooting off after the hook. The sun is getting high, and I am very weary. Stop fishing now. Let's go in. Within a half hour, I am draped over the bow, trying to stay cool and conscious. Finally the massacre is over. It is time for my voyage to end.

LIFE

pull up in front of *Ducky.* I swing my equipment bag over to them. Then they grab me with helping hands and I clamber aboard. I slip into the bottom of the boat and sit among dozens of dorados and a few kingfish and barracuda. I recognize my doggies. There is the one I plucked from the sea—"There, is that what you want, stupid fish!"—simply in order to scare him away. There is the one that bit through my fishing line ahead of the wire. And there is the lovely female that would coyly brush against the raft, always just to the right of where I was aiming. The emerald elders are nowhere to be seen.

I raise myself onto the hard wooden thwarts and rock to one side until I find some flesh on my rear to cushion my pelvis. The men haul the raft aboard the bow, put the helm over, and rev the engine. I nearly fall over backward as we take off. *Ducky* lifts off. The fishermen stop *Clemence,* and I show them where to pull *Ducky*'s plugs. Several gallons of water spurt out of the open valve on the bottom tube while *Ducky* collapses over the bow like a huge black amoeba. She too deserves a rest.

We take off again in island style, with the forty-five-horse Evinrude wide open. The rapid forward progress feels so strange. Waves come up and we rip down them, cleaving the thick water and peeling it to both sides of the boat. We carve a watery line from the Atlantic into the Caribbean. As the boat rolls, the sea blasts by only a few inches from the gunwale. I hope these guys know what they're doing.

Clemence is rustic. The emergency sail is a piece of canvas wrapped around a long stripped sapling. A steel blade, its butt wrapped with cloth and tape, is sheathed in the joints between the boat's planking and frames. The reserve gas tank is a fifteen-gallon plastic jug. When gas runs low, the cap of the jug is pried loose with a piece of rusty rod. The captain, Jules Paquet, sticks a tube in his mouth and sucks fuel up from the reserve. He whips the end out of his mouth and jams it into the engine's tank as he spits a mouthful of gas overboard. We tear off again for a few minutes before the engine quits. Captain Jules pulls the cover off of the Evinrude and begins to diddle with it.

Jules's brother, Jean-Louis, sits beside me. The brothers have sharp noses and dancing eyes. They look Egyptian. Jean-Louis's hair is short, but Jules's is a thick bush that surrounds his head like a halo. Jean-Louis's wide smile is broken amidships by a tiny black cave of missing front teeth. My own smile may never subside.

Paulinus Williams sits behind me. His broad round muscles seem cast in polished iron. His skin is so black that in shadow it's difficult to distinguish his features. His teeth flash as he speaks to me in English while the others discuss the engine in bobbling Creole. Paulinus reassures me. "It is not far to go, maybe one hour."

Clemence jumps into action again. I ask Paulinus what the mountainous island off our bow and beyond this flat one is.

"Guadeloupe is the island there. This one is Marie Galante. Named it is for the ship of Columbus."

So I have gone one better than Guadeloupe. I have landed on the tiny island farthest to the east in the chain, hardly big enough to show up on my chart.

Paulinus yells over the roar of the engine. "You are very lucky. We do not fish on the east of Marie Galante. Only today. We come around and see birds very far away. They fly so far out to sea. We do not fish so far away. But today we decide to go. When we get close we see something. We think that maybe it be a barrel. We go, thinking maybe the dorado swim there. When we get there it is not a barrel. It is you."

As we round Marie Galante to the north, Jules steers *Clemence* close to shore so that she slips down the surge that cracks upon the ancient coral cliffs and then sweeps back out against the incoming swell. The waves blast skyward against the cliffs made by the death of billions of tiny coral animals. The walls are shot full of deep caverns, which echo the boom of Neptune's knock on Mother Earth's door. I envision *Ducky* and me grinding up onto the cliffs, scrambling to grab hold of a small shelf of safety, being beaten down and then dragged off the razor rock.

I begin to sing a favorite song of mine, "Summertime." Now the livin' is so easy. I think of my jumping fish. And on the island the sugar cane will be growing high. I feel free—free enough to spread my wings and reach for the sky. My voice booms out but is lost in the roar of *Clemence* splitting the water and rushing down the waves. Jean-Louis smiles at me and tells me I sing well. Probably not, but I've never felt so in tune with the words. Oh yeah, easy livin'!

The perfume of flowers and grass blows off the island and wafts into my nostrils. I feel as if I'm seeing colors, hearing sounds, and smelling land for the first time. I am emerging from the womb again. The horrible memories of my voyage may haunt me forever, but they are already eased by the ecstasy of a new life and the kindness of these men. For seventy-six days I teetered on the edge of life, afraid to let go, afraid that my own atoms and energy and essence would be lost to my grasp and be used by the universe in whatever way it pleased. Steven Callahan lost without trace.

A strange formation, like an amphitheater, looms before us. Hoya Grande. A large cavern formed and the roof fell in, leaving a tall thin tower of coral open to the sky, and on one side, through the arched aperture, open to the Atlantic.

We round the island and proceed along the leeward west coast. The sea is as flat as a board, the day warm and alive with light and color. A long beach comes into view. Bushy trees and palms shade the small huts and houses clustered under them. It's the village of St. Louis. A number of people are gathered under an unwalled roof held up by corner posts. They quickly notice us. Some stop chatting, others lay down the fish that they are trading. What is that big black blob slung over the bow of *Clemence?* And who is the skinny, bearded white man, nearly as dark as Jules and Jean-Louis, but with sun-frosted hair and snowy brows? Some begin to make their way toward the place where we will land, first slowly, then at a quickened pace.

I look down at the dorados for the last time. Twelve of their kind, twelve triggerfish, four flyers, three birds, and a few pounds of barnacles, crabs, and assorted oceanic booty have kept me alive. Nine ships did not see me. A dozen sharks tested me. Now it is done, finally over, finished. My feelings are as confused as they were that night when I lost *Solo*. It has been so long since I had any reason to be happy that I don't quite know how to handle it. *Clemence*'s bow turns and she scrapes in the sand. I whisper to my fish, "Thank you, my friends. Thank you and good-by."

People trickle down to the beach. Giggling children run up and then stop, eyes wide. The fishermen yell at me to be still, but I make my way forward and swing one leg over the gunwale. I scoot forward so that I'm in shallower water—it would be pretty stupid to fall off and drown six feet from the shore—and lower myself onto what I know is soft white sand, but what feels like a concrete highway swaying in a major earthquake. My eyes seem to be bouncing around like pinballs. I take a step forward and let go of *Clemence*. My head reels. The ground leaps up and crashes against my knees. As my head swings down to hit the beach, two strong men grab my arms from each side and jerk me up to my feet. They lift me up so that my feet barely touch the ground and carry me away. I go through the motions of walking. We pass small tin-walled houses with cleanly cut and brightly painted gingerbread trim. Fish traps are scattered about. Chickens run clucking out of our way. We pass under a shady tree and out onto black pavement. An entourage follows now. On the first corner we come to is a tall yellow building sprouting flags and emblems. The islanders sit me down in a folding metal chair on a shaded porch. Everyone talks at once in a jumble of Creole and French. Finally they get my name and begin making phone calls. I'm left in peace for a moment.

A hundred people press close to the porch. I look at them, unbelieving. It is over. It hits me like a ton of bricks. There are wide eyes, curious eyes, worried eyes, weeping eyes. My own fill with tears, which I try to choke down. I reach through a tangle of arms and grasp the ice-cold ginger beer that is being thrust toward me. These people do not know me. We don't even have a common language. How can they ever know what each step through my hell was like? Yet I have the overwhelming feeling that we belong to one another, that in this moment we see life as one. In their eyes there is a reflection of my own fate. The paths of our lives are separate, but the essence of our lives is together.

I cannot see back to the beach. There, my friends remain in the bottom of *Clemence*. I'll never forget how they flew into the arms of the fishermen, the color and power of their glistening flight. I wonder if out beyond the beach, in the clear blue water, two emerald fish are looking for a new school with whom they will swim, carrying the tale of how simple fish taught a man the intricate mystery that comes with each moment of life.

A
MAN
ALONE

 A VOLKSWAGEN VAN
pulls up in front of the porch. The local constable and a few other men help me inside and we roar off toward the windward side of the island. Everyone is jovial and talkative. I haven't got the vaguest idea what they are saying. One man keeps motioning for me to guzzle my ginger beer. I can't tell him that in the last twelve hours I've had more to drink than I normally consumed in a week in the raft, so I make signs to him and chant, "Slowly, slowly." He nods. Besides, I love holding the cold, wet bottle.

Marie Galante is rather flat. We pass long stretches of sugar cane fields. Ox carts are piled high with cut cane. I cannot believe how sensitive I am to the smells of the cut vegetation, of the flowers, of the bus. It is as if my nerve endings are plugged into an amplifier. The green fields, the pink and orange roadside flowers, practically vibrate with color. I am awash in stimuli.

We come into town and wheel into the parking lot of the Grand Bourg Hospital. Out of white cinderblock buildings, black nurses in white uniforms scurry up, look me over, and disappear. Some gather and talk. Others poke their heads out of the opened windows and watch. A male Caucasian doctor comes down the steps and over to the van. He speaks English. "I am Dr. Dellanoy. What is wrong with you?"

How does one answer that, precisely? "I'm hungry," I tell him. For a while no one seems to know how to deal with me. It is obvious that I am not an emergency case. I explain to Dr. Dellanoy that I have been adrift for seventy-six days and that I'm dehydrated, starved, and weak, but otherwise O.K. He decides to admit me and calls for a stretcher. This seems unnecessary, but I am coerced to climb aboard. When we get upstairs, the stretcher-bearers have trouble getting around the corners in the narrow hallways and I convince them to let me walk. I have developed such effective sea legs that the solid ground feels unstable. The men help me across a portico and into a room, sit me down on a bed, and drop my bag at the foot of it. An old man rises up from the bed opposite me, an intravenous plugged into his arm. We smile at each other.

Dr. Dellanoy comes in and we discuss my condition. My blood pressure is O.K. I've lost about twenty kilos (forty-four pounds), just under a third of my weight. "We'll put you on intravenous feeding and will add some antibiotics to help clear up those sores," he tells me. "Someone in your condition won't be able to eat anything for quite a while, of course—"

"Hang on!" I interrupt him, horrified. "What's that?"

"Your stomach has shrunk. It may be dangerous for you to eat anything solid for some time."

I quickly, desperately explain to him that although I am a tad thin, I've conscientiously eaten as regularly as I can. I'd offer him some fish sticks, but they're back on the raft, wherever poor *Ducky* is. I also don't like the idea of needles and immobilization. "Can't I try to use my mouth?"

"O.K. We'll see how it goes. We'll give you some antibiotic pills, too," he tells me, and then he leaves.

A white nurse arrives. She's roundish and incredibly cheery, with rosy cheeks and a chirpy French voice. Screwing up her face, she pulls off my T-shirt and makeshift diaper, carries them to the corner with two fingers held high, and drops them. Funny, I don't notice any smell. Except for her—she smells clean. She sets down a porcelain basin full of tepid water and begins to wash me. My sores are tender to the rag and her firm, efficient touch, but she is as gentle as she can be, and as she pats me dry I am immediately relieved. Her merry voice never stops. Other nurses pop in and out and chat, or try to chat, with my nurse, the old man, and me. I've never seen such a vivacious hospital.

From the time I hit the beach, I have slowly wound down. After two and a half months, I finally have no fears and no apprehension. There is nothing to do and nothing I want. There is only total rest. I feel like I'm floating. My blond angel finishes and breezes out.

I lay back on the sheets, clean sheets, dry sheets. I can't remember ever feeling like this before, though I imagine that I might have felt this way at birth. I am as helpless as a baby, and each sensation is so strong that it's like seeing, smelling, and touching for the very first time. Heaven *can* exist on earth.

Soon a young man brings in a tray heaped with food. He pours me a large glass of water. For a moment I stare at it all in disbelief. A glass of water. Such a simple thing, a simple treasure. On the tray is a large piece of French bread, a stuffed squash, some vegetables that I don't recognize, roast beef, ham, yams, and in one corner, of all things, a square of salted fish! I almost laugh, but I eat every morsel. Now everyone who comes in and sees the empty tray stares at *me* in disbelief.

I'm given antibiotics and a couple of strong sedatives and am told that I should sleep. Ah yes, sleep. I could sleep for days . . .

Uniformed men suddenly bustle into the room and begin hurling questions at me. Their uniform looks different from that of the police who brought me to the hospital, and it turns out they are the gendarmerie. In the middle of our lengthy interview, there is a phone call for me. An orderly wheels me back across the portico and into one of the doctor's offices, where there is one of the few telephones in the hospital. The call is from Mr. Dwyer, the U.S. consul in Martinique, who extends his welcome to the islands, assures me there will be no problem about my lack of a passport, and extends an offer of any assistance he can render. The news has traveled very quickly. Even as I speak, my mind drifts around sleepily. But back in my room there are more officials and more questions to answer. Finally everyone leaves and I'm left in peace. The old man across from me smiles. I hear dishes clattering in a kitchen below. The breeze blows lightly across my face. A black spiritual sung in a beautiful baritone echoes from the kitchen and through the hospital grounds. I drift off into dreamland.

After a couple of hours I awake, feeling calm. A civilian comes in shyly and sits by my bed. He too looks almost Egyptian. He has a broad smile and speaks a few words of English. I understand that his name is Mathias, that he has a radio station, and that he runs a hotel. I can come and stay in the hotel if I like. He asks what I have with me, and when he sees the bag and my ragged, stinking T-shirt he tells me to wait right here—as if I'm planning on going somewhere—and disappears for an hour.

I pull myself up to a sitting position, grab the railing at the foot of the bed, and gradually stand. My roommate watches me as I wobble about, trying to keep my knees from collapsing. We jovially chat with each other, though neither understands much of what the other is saying.

Mathias returns and spreads out an array of colorful clothes for me: blue pants, bright red shorts, sandals, and a new T-shirt with a map of Marie Galante on it. There is also a bottle of cologne. Maybe I really do reek. I am deeply touched by the generosity of these people. Outside of my room are a number of islanders who have come to see me. They wait patiently, sitting on benches or leaning against the portico railing. I know no one on this island, but I feel as if I'm a long-lost brother who has returned home.

I get up several times and hang on to the bed until I feel pretty confident. The next move is for the door, which is always open. I leap and stumble to it in two steps. Then, hanging on to the rails, I guide myself down the open-air hallway, feeling the breeze, listening to the rustle of the palm fronds, and sucking in the sweet smells. Each step takes a minute, but I'm in no hurry. The nurses watch me but don't interrupt. I think how lucky I am not to be in a stuffy, antiseptic, uptight American institution. Sign language, a few words of French, a few of English, and an intangible spirit go a long way in communicating with the many patients and visitors outside the rooms. I can't believe how relaxed and high-spirited most of them seem.

By early evening the trade winds are cool and a little stronger. I'm dressed and, though tired, anxious to go out on the town. The anesthesiologist at the hospital, Michelle Monternot, has heard of my arrival, and although we have not met she has invited me to her home for dinner this evening. Mathias arrives, followed by two young Frenchmen and a Frenchwoman, who introduce themselves as André Monternot, the anesthesiologist's husband, and Michel and his girlfriend Nanou. They carry an enormous picnic basket, just in case I don't feel up to accompanying them to dinner, but I can't wait to get going. I think I can get across about a hundred feet of open ground by myself, so we make for Mathias's car. I stagger around like a drunk, and I must sound like one, too, because I can't stop laughing hysterically. I guess I'm just intoxicated with being alive.

First we go to Mathias's hotel, where I make some telephone calls. I get through to my parents' house. My brother Ed picks up the phone. "What are *you* doing there?" I ask. "Trying to find out where the hell you've been," he replies jocularly. It seems that my parents have already heard the news. In fact, they knew of my arrival before many of the local authorities. Mathias was among the crowd when I was carried up from the beach, and he immediately sent a message on his CB radio to his friend Freddie in Guadeloupe. Freddie has an amplifier and rebroadcast the message. A man named Maurice Briand was fishing off the coast of Florida when he picked up the signal. He called my parents less than an hour after I stepped ashore. For days I won't believe that this was all possible with CB radios and not ham units, but it turns out to be true. Anyway, my parents are out buying me clothes and making arrangements to come down to the island. But I'm already starting to feel overwhelmed and I suspect that things will be hectic for a few days. Also, I want to be in better shape when they arrive. So I ask my brother if he can convince them to delay their trip. There's no big panic now, I'm safe and secure. I don't know anything about what they've been through in trying to find me. My brother is caught in the middle and tells me he'll do what he can, though he knows they'd hop on a flight tonight if they could.

I will return to Mathias's hotel, Le Salut, tomorrow. Tonight I am regaled by a feast at the Monternots'. Michel turns out to be the customs agent on the island. We joke about my slipshod method of smuggling rafts into Marie Galante. I end up sleeping at the Monternots' house. When I wake up in the morning, I look into the mirror. My God! Who's that? The face I see is straight out of *Robinson Crusoe*. Long, stringy bleached hair, hollow eyes, drawn brown skin, shaggy beard. Michelle Monternot gives me a toothbrush. It feels strange in my mouth. What's even stranger is that my teeth are not crusty and slimy but are remarkably clean. I wonder what my dentist would say about that.

André drives me down to the hospital to collect my things. Upon entering my room, I smell the stink of dead fish. My bag really does reek. Someone's taken the T-shirt, to the nearest rubbish bin, no doubt. A nurse takes my blood pressure again. I check myself out and walk through the gates and into the world, feeling like a free man after a long imprisonment.

Mathias takes me back to his hotel and introduces me to his friend Marie, who speaks English quite well. Throughout my stay they are kind hosts and never balk at the huge quantities of their delicious Creole food that I consume. Everyone is amazed at how much I can pack away.

My parents arrive on an evening flight on the twenty-third. We are reunited after a year, my mother in tears, my father stoical, and me all smiles. So much has passed under my keel in one short year. Yet to them, although I'm a good deal thinner, I am still the same, their son returned.

I am honestly surprised by the fuss that everyone is making over me. Within twenty-four hours I'm giving telephone interviews to English, Canadian, and American reporters. Telegrams arrive. I am debriefed by the French and American Coast Guards and by the police again, and then get my picture taken with the amiable chief. CBS news sends a crew down from Florida. The *National Enquirer* asks me for an exclusive. I decline to give them an interview at all, but that doesn't stop them. They create a fabulous story of how I looked straight into the "glowing amber eyes" of a whale that "roared as only the sea can roar" and smashed my boat again and again. I have yet to see a whale with amber eyes and I've never heard even the slightest croak from one.

When I have a few moments, I try to extend my walks. Within a couple of days, I can do a hundred yards. My legs begin to blow up, as if I have elephantiasis. A local physician, Dr. Lachet, comes by every day to check on me. I feel fortunate because Dr. Lachet has had a lot of experience with starvation in Africa, so he knows what to expect. He runs some tests. I have a very high sodium level, a low potassium level, and I am pretty anemic. My body isn't getting rid of fluids and they are sinking to my legs. I begin taking pills.

I have long, leisurely meals and tour the island. I'm so excited by everything that it's difficult to sleep at night. By dawn I'm awake again and can't wait to get at the world. Instead of resting properly, I get overtired and cranky. People are trying to help me, I realize, but I am beginning to feel my autonomy slip from my grasp. The pressure is getting to me and my temper will probably soon get to everyone else.

My parents try to convince me that I should fly home with them and convalesce. I tell them I can't, that I don't want to be a patient. What I want is to regain my strength here, hitch-hike on boats up to Antigua to collect my mail, and then fly back to Maine.

I spend the next several days getting to know the people of Marie Galante. The bar and restaurant of Hotel Le Salut are open to the street. People often come in to talk. Every few days the fishermen who picked me up stop in. They actually live on Guadeloupe. The day they brought me in, they took their fish home and sold it late into the night. I would like to go out in

Clemence again, perhaps go fishing with them, but it never works out. My walks lengthen. Everywhere I go the islanders stop me. They invite me into their homes or surround me on the street. Those with whom I can speak make jokes about my sure-fire all-fish diet plan. I watch children fill drums with water from spigots that poke up from the sidewalks and roll them home, pushing them with their feet. I feel at ease here, at home. The people of Marie Galante have adopted me.

Some people have started to call me the Super Fisherman or the Superman. I try to explain to them that while I was adrift I kept struggling to survive not because I was heroic but because it was the easiest thing for me to do, easier than dying. One day I am honored by a visit from the local witch doctor. He stares close in my face, his eyes bulging out. He chants a bunch of words, shakes some things around, and looks at me curiously. After he leaves, Mathias tells me who he is and that he has cast a spell to speed my recovery.

The next day I get incredible stomach cramps, develop a high fever, and begin a long bout with diarrhea. For a while I think that I have kidded myself, that I am going to die after all. I ask Mathias not to tell the medicine man about my "recovery." The Creole cooking is excellent, but it is very spicy. Dr. Lachet and Dr. Dellanoy agree that I must lay off the hot peppers for a while. A classic case of way too much way too soon. It's pretty tough for four or five days, but I slowly pull out of it, thanks to the good doctors, my parents, Mathias, and Marie.

I finally recover enough to walk again. I have been on the island ten days. I realize that it is time for me to go. I've met with several sailors. Nick Keig, whom I know of but have never met, arrives with the *Three Legs of Mann IV* and agrees to take me on to Guadeloupe. My parents accept my decision rather well. They help me to get things together, give me money and food treats, and don't try to hold me back. When everything is ready, I hobble down to the concrete pier beside the beach on which *Clemence* delivered *Ducky* and me, lower myself into the

SATISFACTION GUARANTEED—
40% OFF THE COVER PRICE!

ONE YEAR (10 ISSUES) FOR JUST $2.95 AN ISSUE

NAME (PLEASE PRINT)

STREET ADDRESS

CITY / STATE / ZIP CODE

☐ PAYMENT ENCLOSED   ☐ BILL ME

E-MAIL ADDRESS*

THE **Atlantic**

JS0410A

With my saviors: Paulinus Williams and Jules
and Jean-Louis Paquet

With natives of Marie Galante on the beach where I
landed in St. Louis, about a week after I arrived

waiting rubber dinghy, and am shuttled out to the *Three Legs*. I wave good-by to my many friends on the island. I know that I am relaunched into real life. The crew on the *Three Legs* hoist sail, we turn the bow toward Guadeloupe, and I watch my new home recede into the distance.

⟨EPILOGUE

It took me about six weeks to recover to the point of being physically functional. Most of the salt water sores healed before I left Marie Galante. By that time I'd gained back about fifteen pounds, though a good portion of it was in the form of water in my legs and fat in my gut. It took another six weeks for my feet to thin out enough that I could put on shoes and for my weight to return to normal. After several months, my hair began to fall out rapidly. It took two more months for that to subside. Many of the smaller scars on my legs disappeared only after a year. Today there are only a few physical traces left—a variety of scars, a spot in my vision from ramming my eye with the piece of polypropylene. There may be long-term internal damage, but none has shown up yet. The experience did seem to alter my metabolism, however. Before, I normally ate three huge meals each day. Now I can eat a maximum of two meals and often eat only one, plus a snack or two. My weight remains the same.

I have had only one raft-related dream since the voyage began, and no recurring nightmares.

What did I learn from the voyage? My beliefs about the indifference of the sea, about the relative nature of good and evil and of all human values, about the equality of all God's creatures, and about my own insignificance were only reinforced. But I have come to know that the fulfillment of goals is not enough in itself; it must be shared to be rewarding. In addition, I now see that paradoxes in life are common and that making decisions often presents a dilemma, though the decisions are not usually as crucial or as apparent as in a survival situation. Perhaps even more important, knowing starvation and thirst, knowing critical deprivation and desperation first hand, has given me new empathy for the millions on this earth who know nothing else.

The accident has left me with a sense of loss and a lingering fear, but I have chosen to learn from this crisis rather than let it overcome me. Each of us is lucky if we must face only one serious crisis in our lives. And in those times when I feel alone and desperate, I take comfort in the silent company of those who have suffered greater ordeals, and survived.